# THE GRI

Richard Ayoade is a writer and direc̣ ̣ ̣ addition to direct-
ing and co-writing *Garth Marenghi's Darkplace*, he has adapted
and directed Joe Dunthorne's novel *Submarine* for the screen,
and is the co-writer (with Avi Korine) and director of the film
*The Double*. As an actor, he is best known for his roles as Dean
Learner in *Garth Marenghi's Darkplace* and as Maurice Moss
in the Emmy Award-winning *The IT Crowd*, for which he was
awarded a BAFTA for Best Performance in a Comedy.

Richard Ayoade
Presents:

# THE
# GRIP
# OF
# FILM

by
*Gordy LaSure*

FABER & FABER

First published in 2017
by Faber & Faber Limited
Bloomsbury House
74–77 Great Russell Street
London WC1B 3DA
This paperback edition published in 2018

First published in the USA in 2017

Typeset by Ian Bahrami
Printed and bound by CPI Group (UK) Ltd, Croydon, CR0 4YY

A CIP record for this book
is available from the British Library

ISBN 978–0–571–31656–4

2 4 6 8 10 9 7 5 3 1

# CONTENTS

# ANTE FOREWORD BY RICHARD AYOADE

If I've recently learned one thing, it's to never again accept a 'two-book' publishing deal. I've come to realise that I don't have *ideas* as such, and if I *were* to have one, I certainly wouldn't consign it to the anachronistic abstraction of prose. I am technically able to write out words, having attended school most years between the ages of six and nine, but I'm never certain when (or if) they are in the right order.* But as I became more and more celebrated as a visionary filmmaker, my management 'squad' thought it would be wise to fend off the inevitable gush of unauthorised biographies (however flattering) that would soon flood the market. That gushy flood, like in Vol. 1 of the Bible, never happened, but my advance had been cashed, another 'copter was in the hangar and my bleach shares had plummeted. One week later, I delivered the first and final draft of what I wished was my only book. Its title?

*Ayoade on Ayoade: A Cinematic Odyssey.*

The book became an instant bestseller, but the critical response to *AOA: ACO* deeply upset me.** I retreated, wounded, leonine, to one of my Ipswich compounds and immersed myself in the local culture. Two years later, I'd put on thirty pounds and developed a serious lip-salve addiction. At one point my lips were so soft I could barely hold in saliva. I sat dribbling

---

* Or if they're even words! Sometimes they look like demons!
** Eulogies are so limiting – what about the things you *forgot* to praise?

in the town 'centre', plowing through candyfloss while nursing a jumbo isotonic sports drink, its increasingly non-directional sports nozzle foiling my desperate attempts to rehydrate.

Tears, Lucozade and spittle had drenched my jodhpurs. A crowd had gathered.* I had hit Rock Bottom.

My 'mobile' phone sounded, but my hands, tacky with 'floss, could not 'slide to answer'. I had to call back, at my own expense.

                    AYOADE
    Hello?


                NAMELESS PUBLISHER
    Why are you doing a Mick Jagger impression?


                    AYOADE
    Too much lip salve. Who is this?


                NAMELESS PUBLISHER
    It's Walter, your nameless publisher.
    Something interesting's come in. It concerns
    one of those books that tell you how all
    films work.


                    AYOADE
    You mean an A-Z of film? One of the many
    'definitive' tracts that hubristically claim
    to unpack 'long-held principles' of movie
    narrative?


* This was coincidental. A new Greggs was opening and people wanted to taste 'London food'.

NAMELESS PUBLISHER

That's right. We're really excited about it,
but there's a problem.

AYOADE

Hit me.

NAMELESS PUBLISHER

I'd rather tell you - I've temporarily
quelled my desire to strike you.

AYOADE

You're the Nameless Publisher - it's your
pom-pom party.

NAMELESS PUBLISHER

I don't know if that's an obscure reference
or a malapropism.

AYOADE

Welcome to Me.

NAMELESS PUBLISHER

Well, the problem is that the book which
you just defined so concisely is written by
someone that no one's heard of.

AYOADE

Try me. But please don't end a sentence with
a preposition. I'm a serious literary voice.

His name is Gordy LaSure.

That was the first time that I heard the name Gordy LaSure. It wouldn't be the last. Nor the penultimate. Shoot, I wasn't even halfway.

My Nameless Publisher, sensing the aridity of my creative well, was offering me salvation. By 'presenting' Gordy LaSure's book (i.e. writing this Ante Foreword and adding some intermittent, but admittedly prescient, footnotes*), I could rid myself of my contractual obligation and settle most of my dry-cleaning bills. But what started as a 'job for hire' turned into an opportunity to drink both personally, intimately and greedily from the private fountain of a master. I'd like to thank Gordy for engorging *my* well, and for wetting its perimeter with his uniquely salty waters.

But this isn't my book, it's Gordy's.** So let's hear a little more about him . . .

* Please note that from now on, my [Ayoade's] footnotes will be signed '*Ayo*'.
** Except w/r/t royalties, which are split more or less equally – *Ayo*.

# FOREWORD BY SKIPPY BRISKMAN

Gordy LaSure wouldn't want this introduction. He cares too much about directness, plainness and integrity to have Some Notable uncase his drum brushes and start giving it the Big Soft Roll. No, Gordy LaSure would sooner pull out his thick penis and piss on a plaudit than waste a single one of his Few Remaining Goddam Minutes prizing one. Not for Gordy LaSure the shrill hiss of hype, the tinny clang of gongs, the flaccid rim of flattery. When the spotlight arcs into life, distilling its dazzle down onto the stage, you're more likely to see the shifting cirrus of Gordy LaSure's dust than The Man Himself. You'll find him, if you can get a seat, at one of his seminars, where his eager students await his piercing insights on film structure. Gordy literally and legally owns that room, his wise eyes shadowed by a forehead rammed full of insight, his expressive arms sinewed from a lifetime of tearing down expectations. And if, after Gordy LaSure flings out a stack of his legendary lecture notes, you're foolish enough to Blow Smoke Up Gordy LaSure's Ass, he'll tell you how that particular expression refers to the eighteenth-century practice of rectally resuscitating the near-victims of drowning. Don't believe him? Wait till he whips out his copper-nozzled bellows!

Gordy LaSure sure as *hell* wouldn't want this introduction. 'Fuck you!' I can hear him say. 'Get the hell off my property, you no-neck fuck! I don't care how many Oscars you've won.'*

---

* None – *Ayo*.

And I would scramble through his Tibetan Peace Garden and Work-Out Center,* taking refuge behind the newly installed Lat Pull Down while he drunkenly fumbled with his Luger.

Let's be as clear as a disinfected mountain river: Gordy LaSure fucking *hates* introductions. 'Wanna know how to write a good scene? Show up as late as you can, then get the hell out of there.' And he's right. Ain't nothing worse than a piece-of-shit Foreword.**

But – and here's the dumb-fuckery of it all – Gordy LaSure *needs* an introduction. Not because he's an unknown. On the contrary, his name is whispered with awed approbation by studio heads, filmmakers and his remaining students, all paying witness to his unbridled brilliance, his relentless perspicacity and, before a minor operation on his glands, his persistent perspiration. Gordy LaSure's passionate about film. He eats film, he drinks film and sometimes he'll even *watch* a film. But most of all he loves *talking to people* about film, whether a comely student with low confidence and a father complex, a studio 'development' exec who doesn't trust his own judgment, or the countless people Gordy LaSure's encounters in his capacity as the web moderator on an Excessive Sweating Discussion Forum. Gordy LaSure's *always* talking about films and how they'd be a shit-ton better if only people would pull their asses out of their ears and listen to Gordy LaSure.

Let's throw up a few of his achievements from his tenure at the South Los Angeles Drop-In Center (a place that he's transformed from a glorified Vegetarian Taco Stand to the vibrant, if necessarily transient, community it is today). Thus far Gordy's founded the Critical Film Study Doctorate Program; the Film

* This isn't Gordy's property; this is a park that he sometimes collapses in – *Ayo.*
** Speak for yourself, Skippy! – *Ayo.*

as Text Doctorate Program; the Text Can't Be Film Until Filmed Program; the Society for the Study of Film in Society Program; the School of Film, Theater, Television, and Other Formerly Relevant Media Program; and the Red Meat Only Taco Stand. Not too shabby for a Limey Son of a Bitch from Glasgow, England.

But he's left his true legacy in, and sometimes on, the body of his students. Gordy LaSure has taught over thirty thousand different classes at SLADIC, and he's dished out a hell of a lot of meaty tacos. Countless men, women and vagrants have attended his all-night seminars where, fueled by peppery beef, consensual neck rubs and the music of Tony Bennett, he eulogizes long into the night over film and film structure, pausing only to vomit or manage his dwindling property portfolio. Indeed, his understanding of every aspect of movie storytelling is so masterful it's surprising that he's never written a script himself.

What he has written, in copious quantities, are handouts. This book is a compilation of a lifetime of handouts. Handouts that are hand-crafted, hand-picked and hands-on. They're fecund with concepts, observations and something that this Town gets a little scared by: Ideas. What this book doesn't give a Solitary Goddam about are Rules. Gordy LaSure hates Rules more than a dry freshman party. What he loves are Time-Proven Principles of Infinite Scope that Resist Easy Summation. He calls these TPPOISTRES.

Having said that (and he's gonna say it himself, again and again), the voyage of this book can be categorized as an attempt (and a superlatively successful one at that) to understand How in Hell Film Works. Why are some films bad and some films *terrible*? How come just a handful of films (*Titanic*, *Porky's*, *Dirty Harry*) are *any good at all*? Gordy'll tell you How and Why.

Then he'll give you a slug of Wherefore on the side. And he doesn't just shoot from the hip; he shoots from the gut.

I could hurl adjectives at Gordy LaSure – 'provocative', 'witty', 'independent', 'contrary', 'taut' – but he'd only grab them and stuff them right up the new one he'd torn me, so I'll restrict myself to the following: Gordy LaSure is an Enabler. Just as you're forever grateful to the dealer who sold you your first gateway drug, so you'll be forever indebted to Gordy LaSure. Has a man ever had such scope? (He's as likely to riff on quantum mathematics or on how to unclasp a bra when you've lost all feeling in your upper body as he is on Aristotle the Greek.) Has a man ever had such heart? (His cardiologist had to specially enlarge Gordy LaSure's ribcage.) Has a man ever had such balls? (He has a paternity attorney on retainer.) Gordy LaSure brings his gifts of Scope, Heart and Balls to each one of these pages, transporting you, elevating you, *enabling* you. Unabashedly personal, unashamedly polemical, this is Gordy LaSure as he'd show up to your apartment – angry, red-faced and in the raw.

I would not recommend trying to read this book in one sitting. In fact, I wouldn't even recommend you *sit* when you're reading Gordy LaSure. You should be standing tall in an open-top Cadillac, roaring down Route 66, book in one hand, bottle of Jack in the other, your best gal at the wheel and Hollywood in your sights. Or maybe you should be striding across a drifting glacier, stripped to the waist with a bellyful of peyote. Or maybe you should flick through for a quick five in the brief recovery period before Round Two.

For those who know him, this book is a reconfirmation of his genius. For those who don't, it will be a revelation, a bolt from the deep beyond, a *sine qua non* of cinema. But, above all, it'll be an introduction to a lifetime of discovery. Hold up. What word did I just use? Oh yeah: 'introduction'. You see, Gordy. I *said* you needed one . . . Now put down the Luger . . .

Skippy Briskman

Four Times Academy Award-Nominated Producer

Los Angeles, 2017

# INTRODUCTION

I'm flattered and humbled to my inner core by the kind words of Skippy Briskman. Briskman's sharper than my momma's tongue, and goddam it if the son of a bitch ain't always right.

I *fucking detest* introductions.

But what I *don't* hate the shit out of is that for the past thirty years and change I've taught nearly thirty-one thousand separate 'under the counter' diploma courses at SLADIC, while working butt to butt with some of the most talented people ever to set foot on soil. Every day I've been challenged, invigorated and occasionally washed by the most vital student body on the planet. And when our paths again cross, whether in court or on the campus, my former pupils always ask the same two things: (1) 'Why can't we get documentation?' (2) 'When are you going to marshal your myriad insights into a book?' And while I never ran out of excuses for the first question, the second one started to eat at me. This book is their fault as well as mine.

But when I sat down to write it, I recalled the mantra I mutter to myself at every new-student mixer: pull the ripcord before all the good ass has left the party. No one wants to see you half-cut and cab-less, arguing with three dudes too stoned to get their iPod off Repeat One.

So I've tried to make this book as dense as possible, like a neutron star. And if you think I came up with that simile by googling 'What stuff is most dense?', you'd be wrong. I already knew neutron stars were maybe dense before I googled it to make sure.

And while everyone who's read this book has said they inhaled it in one deep, life-affirming breath, it wasn't written to be consumed as such. Like with a lot of French films, you won't find much in the way of *narrative* here. Treat this book as a map – albeit alphabetical – running the full girth of those twenty or so primal letters, a schema of uncharted movie territory for those times when you wonder why movies take a hold of us, often in the dark, and refuse to let go. Those are the moments when you know you're in . . .

. . . The Grip of Film.

But before film makes one almighty fist, I've gotta coupla fellas to thank . . .

# ACKNOWLEDGMENTS

No man is an island,* just as no man is an inlet; and, unless I was too drunk to download the attachment, no man is Ireland. Though Terry Wogan came close. Men are pretty much just carbon, nitrogen, hydrogen, oxygen and balls. But gas and balls will only get you so far in this Town.

You need a butt-ton of buddies.

You need a tight-knit cadre of hombres and hombresses whose appreciation for wind and piss is about two clicks west of COULDNTGIVEASHITSVILLE. A squad of stone-faced killers who, no matter how sweet you sugar that particular brand of horseshit you're cooking up, ain't in the business of letting you ladle out a bowl.

You need you some Go-To Guys.

Sometimes I Go-To them for solace. Sometimes I Go-To them for shelter (I have a penchant for putting bullets through the roof as punctuation points). But most times I Go-To them because I ain't got no place else to Go-To.

These are the Guys who, when I'm lubed up and lonely, let me inhale a gallon of peach cobbler straight from their freezer. These are the Guys who, when I'm all out of banana polish and hand sanitizer, will fork-lift me off their porch and jump-lead me back to consciousness. These are the Guys who, when I'm

---

* Equally, no man is a cattle grid, but I guess you can only have one image per aphorism – *Ayo*.

being an ass jacket, tell me, 'Gordy, you're being an ass jacket. You've got to stop breaking into our house. We have children now.'

To RUSTY FLANNEL. Rusty initially entered my life as an oral hygienist but, before the appointment was even partway through, segued into both bereavement counselor and bunk-up buddy. As we finished off our second gas canister, she voluntarily offered to look through some of my own writing. Next morning, I was told she had unexpectedly relocated. Just knowing she's potentially somewhere close to me, and might possibly be reading if not actively returning my emails, is a tremendous comfort and support.

To MUSTAFA AXELROD – what you did to my back was beyond words. Without your prolonged brutality, I might never have found the time to write.

To LANCE CORPORAL COLLINS, who taught me most of what I know about mercy, and when it's okay to withhold it.

To my ex-wife CANDY CANYONS, who taught me that love *is* absolutely conditional, and that sometimes those conditions need to be stipulated in advance.

To my ex-wife MISTY MOUNTAINS, for making me realize how much I needed to be free.

To my ex-wife SALTY DELTA, who, on several occasions, convinced me that evil has an actual face.

To my ex-wife KIMBERLY KNIMBLE, who taught me that there's more to life than just being blindly loyal.

To my manager MOTOLA DELUCA, who has shown me that everything on earth *is* reducible to a dollar value.

To my legal team at AGELMAN AND AGLEMAN, who gave me the courage to experiment with my nasal hair.

To ANNE FARTE – what this dame don't know about layout ain't worth knowing. Not that I even know what layout is, but I think it's something to do with gaps. Come to think of it, maybe what I mean to say is, it ain't worth laying out unless you're laying Farte (if you catch my drift).

To PETIE POWELL, one of Harvard's youngest-ever graduates, who then got old like the rest of us. A former pupil of mine, his pedantry is only matched by his distaste for breath mints. But his voluminous notes were rarely just vindictive, and must have helped in some way.

To MY CURRENT WIFE – whoever she may be at time of print.

Rusty, Mustafa, Lance, Candy, Salty, Kimberly, Motola, Agelman, Agleman, Fartie, Petie, Current Wifie: I salute you all. Without you, no *Grip of Film*.

Lastly, and legally, I'm obliged to thank Richard Ayoade, to whom I 'told' this. Here's to you, you glorified typist. I'll always remember your taking 20 per cent from a broke bum. Why don't you try coming up with something yourself, you plagiarizing stack of fuck?*

---

* Mixed feelings about this, and I don't want to get all legal so early. Suffice to say, the final figure's closer to 60 per cent, so draw your own conclusions about the scale of my contribution – *Ayo*.

– xxii –

# WHAT THE HELL AM I READING EXACTLY?

This is a book about how, why, when and if films *work*. The meanings of 'how', 'why', 'when' and 'work' are pretty clear, but the terms 'if' and 'films' could use a little clarification. Let's cut the deck.

'If' is used here in a similar way to the word 'whether'. It's conditional, people. I'm saying that films *might* not make ANY sense. I think it's unlikely, but it's useful to bear it in mind, even though it's definitely best to completely ignore it. Otherwise we could all be wasting our time. And if we are – and that's totally possible, if not probable – we should absolutely just ignore that too. The other important thing to keep up front and center stage – and why the word 'if' is so important to me – is that I don't want to be held responsible *if* in the future (e.g. next month/a month subsequent to that) a group of people can actually *prove* that films don't work/are a waste of time (e.g. there's been an evolutionary leap in intelligence because of something nuclear). Because if *that happens*, I don't want to be this big pro-film blowhard going, 'Hey, look how well films work, everyone!!' I can totally imagine a world where someone like a Dickie Dawkins or that guy who invented the Dyson manages to scientifically prove that films don't work/exist. But what I am *also saying* is that I *believe* that there *are* such things as 'films' and *some* of them 'work'. Maybe. But I'm *not* saying that *my* reality is the only one that *could* exist. I'm massively signed up to the multiverse. And in that respect I'm completely with Scott

Bakula. I think that quantum shit is just as valid as real-time shit. I don't know if this makes sense – I'm a little jacked – but I just want to be honest, as well as pre-emptively defend myself because I'm so fucking sick of being attacked right now I could strangle someone.

'Films': what the fuck are films? Easy, padre – holster your blaster – because you're holding my 320-page answer. So let's not flip our lids just yet. But what I can say for certain(ish) is that I sure as shit know *where* films are. They're in America. Fact is, the reason I shipped out from Glasgow back before beyond (besides some mixed feelings w/r/t unprovoked head-butting) was because I wanted to be where *movies were*. And that's Way Out West. You know the place – they say 'hooray' for it. Still lost? Then glance up at the big-ass sign . . . I'm talking about H-O-L-L-Y-W-O-O-D. This is a Town that's consti-tutionally committed to clarity. In 45ft-high letters. And (if you want to talk cultural significance) those letters matter so much in these parts that Hugh Hefner, the international face of non-penetrative pornography, put his hand down his silk pyjamas to pony up for the restoration of the letter 'Y': the letter that looks most like the thing he's dedicated his life to not quite showing.

So let's call a dick a dick: when I talk about films, I'm not talking about *Werner the Elephant*, an elegiac tone poem by some architecture postgrad from Portugal. I'm talking about films made in this Town. Films that *actual* people *actually* want to see. They're popular. They're important. They're immortal. And *The Grip of Film* is only gonna pick the juiciest fruit from the bush. So go kneel on a splash mat – your cup's about to overflow. This is the kind of thing I'm talking about when I talk about film . . .

Roll call!

*3 Days to Kill*
*Above the Law*
*The Avengers*
*Bangkok Adrenaline*
*Bangkok Dangerous*
*Barb Wire*
*Basic Instinct*
*Beverly Hills Cop*
*Body of Evidence*
Bond films
*Captain Ron*
*Charlie's Angels II: Full Throttle*
*Click*
*Cocktail*
*Cop and a Half*
*Cop Out*
*Crank*
*A Dangerous Man*
*Die Hard*
*The Equalizer*
*Executive Decision*
*Fire Down Below*
*Freddie Got Fingered*
*Ghost Dad*
*Ghosts of Girlfriends Past*
*Hard to Kill*
*He's Just Not That into You*
*Highlander*
*Hotel for Dogs*
*I Now Pronounce You Chuck & Larry*
*It's Complicated*

*Jaws: The Revenge*

*Just Go with It*

*Kindergarten Cop*

*Legally Blonde*

*Look Who's Talking*

*Mall Cop*

*The Man from U.N.C.L.E.* (Guy Ritchie version)

*Marked for Death*

*Meet Dave*

*Olympus Has Fallen*

*Predator*

*Raw Deal*

*Red Scorpion*

*Red Sonja*

*Road House*

*RoboCop*

*Rocky*

*Shanghai Surprise*

*Showgirls*

*Silent Rage*

*Six Bullets*

*Sliver*

*Striptease*

The *Taken* trilogy

*The Terminator*

*Timecop*

*Tokarev*

*Total Recall*

Michael Bay's *Transformers* (quadrilogy)

*View from the Top*

*What Happens in Vegas*

*What to Expect When You're Expecting*
*White Chicks*
*Young Guns II: Blaze of Glory*

I make no apology for the fact that many of these films are from the eighties. As far as I'm concerned, that's the last decade when kicking butt and taking names was what this Town *did*. And what names! Some of the most pumped-up dudes ever to walk past a phalanx of felled flunkies. Stand-up guys, standing tall in concealed lifts. Cruise, Lundgren, Russell, Stallone, Van Damme. Artists. Storytellers. Icons. Each one has held me and countless others in *Film's Grip*, both on and off camera. I also make no apology for the fact that I've seen no more than eight of the films on this list. But I sure as hell plan to. Especially *White Chicks*, which sounds super-sexy and really not that racist.

Films are stories, and stories are 'equipment for living'. Recent scientific studies have confirmed that we now need movies more than we need food. In fact, they have shown that mice deprived of stories end up eating themselves, or at the very least *eating more than they should*.

So, to study such films is to make a study of our own hearts. Not as the black husk we dimly discern when we let some light in under the duvet (appropriately called 'comforters' on these shores), but as we'd like our hearts to be: open, healthy and free from atherosclerosis.

To spend time with movies such as these is to find out what makes us who we are, and why we need to gather in the dark and tell one another our deepest dreams, desires and high-speed-chase survival stories.

Interested?

Then stop yanking it and come on in.

# A NOTE ON THE TEXT

Much of this text has been cut without my permission.* As a result, little of it makes sense, and some parts have ended up flat-out racist. Often passages end with a cross-reference to another passage that has been omitted, but some passages seem the same as before the cuts (or even longer, if that's possible?) – I can't really tell anymore, I'm so tired of fighting these goddam book people with their 'grammar' and intolerance for 'repetition'.

Upshot?

I'm as frustrated with this situation as you're about to be.

---

* This is simply untrue. All cuts were made after a rigorous (email) consultation process. LaSure had final say, but he would often refuse to *say* anything. He would answer most of my enquiries by sending me a picture of his penis. However, for some reason he insisted on keeping in the references to the pieces that were cut. Why? Who knows? The only explanation I could hazard is our old friend 'Word Count'. LaSure is a pamphlet man. If you cut him open, you'd snag your blade on a couple of cheap staples – *Ayo*.

## A NOTE ON THE USE OF GENDER
## WITHIN THE TEXT

I'm a man and I'm sick of apologizing for it.

I'm sick of standing in front of some tribunal and having to explain that what I did is *normal male behavior.* And yes, you *can* sue me. That *is* your right. And, in fact, you *are currently suing me*, but *this is who I am.* You *knew* I couldn't be faithful. I *work* with *women*! What did you expect me to do? Just look at them?!

Point is, I'm not going to transition. I'm not ready to hand in my 'Y' chromosomes to the Matriarchy. I'm not saying I'm done talking to women. I'm just saying I'm assuming they're done talking to me. I'm a Man's Man, and for the sake of this book I'm going to assume you are too. In fact, as long as you're between these here covers, you're *my* Man.

So sure, break my balls for writing 'him' rather than 'him/ her'. Kick me in the ass for trying to write elegant. Do you know how tempting it was to write 'him/her' seeing as I *barely made my contractual word count*?

I'll answer you.

It was tempting.

It was very tempting.

It was very, very tempting.*

But I'm an artist. I go *my* way. And that's the way of an Ethnically Non-Diverse Cisgender Dude.

---

* I fought and I fought and I fought.

Ready for some straight shootin'?
Cos I've got a full clip, baby.

# DISCLAIMER

You may think, seeing as we're already thirty pages deep and the book hasn't even got going, that I'm having a problem with startin' her up.

Sure. It's no longer a certainty.

But you try maintaining a loving physical relationship when you don't have a regular roof over your head. Most places I stay, I don't own. Most places I stay, I'm not meant to be there. In fact, let's call an ass an ass: most places I stay, I've *forced entry*.

So yeah, if they've installed an alarm system, we *will* have to get down to it in the jeep. And that vehicle has all my stuff piled up on the passenger seat, including my lecture notes, which don't have plastic covers anymore because I wanted to see how easily they'd melt, so okay, we're just gonna have to head on out to the flatbed.

Al fresco.

Come rain, come shine.

And let's get some intel on this: the back of my jeep doesn't even have a *cover*. The tarpaulin on the deck is *rancid*. Sometimes the smell is so strong I forget why I'm even *there*. And by the time I've scrubbed down and made good, the moment's long gone.

So's she.

What're you gonna do? The gun range is closed for the night and your limp's pretty bad now.

Best grab a drink from the dash and take in a movie, huh?

# THE GRIP OF FILM

## AN A–W* OF MOVIES

---

* Gordy wanted to be upfront about the fact that he couldn't think of a 'single, goddam thing beginning with "X", "Y" or "Z"' – *Ayo*.

*'We're born; we live; we die . . .'*

# ACTION

Guess what the director shouts at the start of every take? I'll give you a clue: it ain't 'Talk!' Whoever heard of Talkies!?

You SLUG the guy.
You KISS the dame.
You TOTAL the car.

That's movies.*

And I love 'em.

See: KISSING; SLUGGING; TOTALING

* A similar order of events unfolded when I accompanied Gordy on a taco tour of Montana. At one point he tried to rip off my arm because he thought I was a chicken fajita. LaSure would often go into deliriums precipitated by hand sanitiser, which he would drink when he ran out of nail-polish remover – *Ayo*.

# ACT STRUCTURE

We're born; we live; we die.

How's that for a THREE-ACT STRUCTURE?*

All successful movies have three acts: Act I, Act IIA, Act IIB and Act III (not incl. the EPILOGUE). To highlight these Aristotelian principles in even more depth, let's lock eyes once more on John Irvin's visionary 1986 action thriller *Raw Deal*.

## ACT I

A Mob informant under FBI protection is hiding out in the woods when – BAM! – an elite hit squad turns this 'safe' house into a 'not-so-safe' house. One of the fresh cadavers is Blair Shannon, the kid of FBI agent Harry Shannon (Darren McGavin). Surveying the aftermath, Shannon senior is busted up: 'Thirty-seven years of this shit and I never got a scratch . . . They're dead, whoever set this up. Whatever it takes, they're dead.' The subtext? Shannon wants payback. And then some.**

*Cut to*: Small-town sheriff Mark Kaminsky (Arnold Schwarzenegger) taking down some punk posing as a motorcycle cop. After

---

* I really don't want to be a pedant, but this isn't a dramatic structure at all. Birth and death are relatively short, even in their most protracted forms. What we're left with is an ungoverned blob between these two generally unsolicited events – *Ayo*.

** What? Supplementary payback? A city break? – *Ayo*.

he busts the sorry lowlife, he goes home to his PAIN-IN-THE-ASS WIFE. This broad drinks like an open gutter, and what's more, she's slamming the hard stuff. We instantly know she's a BAD PERSON and unlikely to feature heavily in this narrative, except as an OBSTACLE. During their drunken row, we hear Kaminsky's BACKSTORY.

Kaminsky was run out the Bureau by a PEN-PUSHING SON OF A BITCH called Marvin Baxter (Joe Regalbuto), when all Kaminsky had done was shake down a piece of shit who'd iced a kid. If Kaminsky hadn't resigned, Baxter would have prosecuted and Kaminsky might not have got his current crappy sheriff's job, which – by the way – he's pretty damn good at, not that his wife gives a fuck. In fact, this sodden wreck tries to hit him in the kisser with a chocolate cake that has the word 'SHIT' written on it in squirty cream. As an audience, we instantly know that she's pissed as hell, and possibly didn't even enjoy making the cake. She's doesn't know how lucky she is that her husband has provided a *roof* over her drunk head AND an oven so she can make these sarcastic gestures in the first place! She misses Kaminsky by a mile. 'You should not drink and bake,'* Kaminsky fires back, sharp as a whip.

Later, when the old soak has passed out, Kaminsky, displaying the kind of largesse that binds us to him for ever, picks up this sloshed harlot in his safe, manly-as-hell arms and puts her to bed. Movies help us understand that people who can't function

* Is this meant to be a saying? Or a pun? 'Bake' doesn't sound anything like 'drive'. If she had been intoxicated while jumping head first into a swimming pool, Schwarzenegger would have had a better chance of a choice rejoinder. But you feel that, even then, he would probably have said, 'You should not drink and then jump head first into a pool' – *Ayo*.

after consuming large amounts of alcohol are despicable bums. Kaminsky can handle his drink – it's one of the many things that make him better than other people and worthy of the CAMERA'S CONSTANT LOVING GAZE.

But before he even gets a chance to unwind with a slug of the good stuff, he receives a telephone call from his old colleague Harry Shannon. Thus the CALL TO ACTION in Gary DeVore and Norman Wexler's clever screenplay (from a story by Luciano Vincenzoni and Sergio Donati) is brilliantly literalized into an *actual call.* Shannon needs Kaminsky to go undercover and tear the Mob a new one. If Kaminsky successfully exacts revenge for Shannon's son, he'll have a shot at re-entering the Bureau.

So, after a brief REFUSAL OF THE CALL (Kaminsky, characteristically humble: 'There's nothing that a small-town sheriff can do that you can't'), Shannon REFUSES THE REFUSAL OF THE CALL by saying that this is under-the-radar shit, totally on the lowdown, and no one else is close to badass enough. Kaminsky uses the HERO'S PREFERRED VERBAL MODE OF ASSENT: the quip. 'Do you think I'll still pass the physical?' Of course he'll pass the physical! His tits are like marble!

So Kaminsky fakes his own death in a CHEMICAL PLANT EXPLOSION and re-emerges with a new identity: convicted felon Joseph P. Brenner. The audience's nuts are in their stomachs. There's no turning back. We're ASS DEEP into –

ACT IIA

Brenner/Kaminsky cosies up to Paulo Rocca (Paul Shenar), the right-hand man to head hombre Luigi Patrovita (Sam

Wanamaker), convincing him they need a BADASS like him on their side by shaking down their rivals and generally being tough as shit. It's while at Patrovita's secret basement casino that he meets Monique (Kathryn Harrold), a high-class piece who works for Rocca's top-level flunky Max Keller (Robert Davi). It's clear that she immediately wants him inside her on account of his being a PRIME PIECE OF BEEF WHO CAN HANDLE A HOT TAMALE. Kaminsky fast becomes a Mob linchpin, recovering $100 mil of China White from the Feds, as well as ghosting a rival hood. But Keller manages to find out that Kaminsky is not who he says he is and rats him out.

ACT IIB

Meanwhile, we find out the original leak was Baxter – the yellow piece of shit that ran Kaminsky outta the Bureau in the first place! When Kaminsky and Keller go to a cemetery to perform a routine hit, the target is revealed to be Shannon, blowing Kaminsky's cover. Together they manage to mow down Keller and another Mob goon, but Shannon gets hurt real bad in the crossfire. Kaminsky gets out by the skin of his butt and takes Monique (who basically loves him now) to the airport. He tells her to wait for him while he embarks on some MAN'S BUSINESS . . .

. . . AN EXTENDED ACT III ASS-KICK.

ACT III

Kaminsky suits up, tools up and single-handedly lays waste to every rotten fuck stationed at Patrovita's gravel pit, wherefrom he swipes a mountain of green. He then heads to Patrovita's casino and executes the louses who offed Blair. He then kills, in order, Rocca, Patrovita and Baxter, before heading to the airport to give Monique a cool quarter mil in readies. He tells her to take off and start again, even though the chances of her meeting a man of his caliber are two clicks west of Not Fucking Likely.

EPILOGUE

Kaminsky visits Shannon at a rehab center and forces him to walk by shouting at him and telling him not to be such a goddam baby.

* * *

So what have we learned about structure? Well, if you pull your dick out your ear and listen up: E-V-E-R-Y-T-H-I-N-G. Let's analyze this mother.

ACT I . . .

. . . is where you start her up. We meet the main actor, find out what 'character' he's pretending to play this time, finger the assholes in his way, discover which dame's gonna be sticking her damn beak in and whose ass he'll need to kick at the end of Act III. At some point during Act I our HERO will do something that means he'll need to leave his ZONE OF COMFORT. And I ain't talkin' 'bout your momma's house – I'm talkin' 'bout A HUGE CHANGE THAT'S ACTUALLY PRETTY MAJOR. In *Deal* it's when Kaminsky fakes his own death at the chemical plant, something I've only had to do twice. At this point the protagonist CANNOT GO BACK. In this way, each one of my divorces has been a HERO'S JOURNEY.

## ACT IIA . . .

. . . shows the hero getting used to his new role. This often involves TRAINING MONTAGES. After some initial awkwardness, he starts to ACE SHIT LIKE A BADASS, until something unexpected happens that makes things ALL FUCKED UP. This is the mid-point, the part of the movie where things are at their most 'mid'. In *Deal*, it's when a cowardly flunky blows Kaminsky's cover.

## ACT IIB . . .

. . . is a bunch of shit going south, and just like life, the middle part is a son of a gun.* Long, boring, aimless – you can't get through it sober. Finally, you get to the point where you can't take it anymore, so you MAN UP AND START ACTING LIKE A BOSS.

## ACT III . . .

. . . is the final ASS-KICKING RAMPAGE, which culminates in a specific, HIGH-LEVEL ASS-KICK OF A TOUGH MOTHERFUCKER. As such, before we go full tilt, the hero needs to . . .

TOOL UP – stash guns in boots/holsters/holdalls; feed a ton of bullets into bullet belts; strap knives to himself, etc.

SUIT UP – leather jacket/shades. (Not actual suits, unless it's a courtroom drama, like *Legally Blonde*.)

MAN UP – e.g. a SLOW-MOTION POWER STRIDE toward

---

* I've always assumed that a son of a gun would be an initially smaller gun, a plucky little pistol, always getting into scrapes – *Ayo*.

THE ULTIMATE SITE OF ASS-KICKING. If the story concerns a MULTIPLE-HERO TEAM, like *Charlie's Angels: Full Throttle*, then it's advisable to have at least one scene where they SLO-MO STRIDE IN A LINE.

TRACK DOWN AND EXECUTE A BUNCH OF ASS-HOLES. Note: (barbed) put-downs regarding previous conduct should only be exchanged with NAMED CHARACTERS.

THE EPILOGUE . . .

. . . ties up outstanding plot holes. (Dealing with them earlier would have interfered with the rhythm of the EXTENDED ASS-KICK.) It's also an opportunity for everyone to THANK THE HERO for being so selflessly great throughout.

So that's structure, fuckers.* All you gotta do is put some meat on dem bones.

See: ASS DEPTH; ASS-KICKING, ULTIMATE SITE OF; ASS-KICKS, EXTENDED ACT III; BACKSTORY; BAD PEOPLE; BADASS, ACING SHIT LIKE A; CALL TO ACTION (AS AN ACTUAL CALL); CALL, REFUSAL OF THE; CALL, REFUSING THE REFUSAL OF THE; CHANGES THAT ARE ACTUALLY PRETTY MAJOR, HUGE; CHEMICAL PLANT EXPLOSION, FAKING DEATH BY PRECIPITATING A; DIALOGUE WITH THEM, CHARACTERS HAVING A NAME BEING A PREREQUISITE OF ENGAGING IN; FUCKEDUPNESS, MID-POINT AS APEX OF; HERO, THE; HERO'S INHERENT

---

* I'm no prude – I'll leaf through *GQ* magazine if I'm waiting at the dentist – but I do find the relentlessness of Gordy's profanity exhausting. It's like he's *sponsored* by the word 'fuck' – *Ayo*.

SUPERIORITY, CAMERA'S LOVING GAZE AS INDICATION
OF; HOT TAMALES, PRIME PIECE OF BEEF'S ABILITY
TO EASILY HANDLE; LINES, STRIDING FORWARD
PURPOSEFULLY IN; MANNING UP, ACTING LIKE A BOSS
AS A WAY OF; MAN'S BUSINESS; OBSTACLE, WOMAN
AS; PAIN-IN-THE-ASS WIVES; POWER STRIDES, SLOW-
MOTION; RAMPAGES, ASS-KICKING; SONS OF BITCHES,
PEN-PUSHIN'; THANKING THE HERO, IMPORTANCE OF;
TOUGH MOTHERFUCKER, HIGH-LEVEL ASS-KICKING OF
A; TRAINING MONTAGES; VERBAL MODES OF ASSENT,
HERO'S PREFERRED; ZONES YOU'RE NOT ALLOWED TO
TAKE COMFORT FROM

# ACTORS, AMATEUR

Every so often an 'auteur' will use AMATEUR ACTORS in a film. They'd have you believe it makes things more 'authentic'.

Italian neo-realism was one such nadir. Suddenly, every fisherman with sad eyes was thumbing a ride to Casting Centrale. But these boner-killing fads never last long.

One of the reasons *The Avengers* is among the highest-grossing films of all time is that it's filled with people *who act for a living*. They don't care whether the dialogue makes any sense! For the correct fee, they'll pretend it does!

This is their *career*.

'Loki, turn off the Tesseract or I'll destroy it' is a line that can only be said by a professional. An amateur wouldn't be able to make it halfway through without laughing.

See: TURNING OFF A TESSERACT (TO PREVENT ITS DESTRUCTION)

## ACTORS, HAVING MORE THAN
## ONE ASIAN ONE

Will there ever be a Hollywood film starring more than one Asian person?

Maybe if every non-Asian actor dies. And if the cost of revivifying those dead non-Asian actors is prohibitive.

Some people are gonna cry 'racism'. Well, cry me a river and meet me down the delta of DontGiveAFuck.

Not hiring people because of their race is a constitutional right. That's one of the reasons I came to this country.

Should I go to jail because I don't trust Caucasians to do valet parking? Apparently, yes. And I have.

The fact that Hollywood won't hire Asian people except as background players clustered round a computer has precisely jack shit to do with typing, let alone stereos.

Fact is, the only stereo type I'll even *think* about buying is a Yamaha.

And *I'm* the racist?

Please.

See: REVIVIFICATION, ACCURATELY COSTING; VALET PARKING, QUESTIONABILITY OF CAUCASIANS' ABILITY TO SUCCESSFULLY PERFORM

# ADR

ADR stands for AUTOMATED DIALOGUE RECORDING. It refers to the process by which a filmmaker may re-record lines of dialogue after shooting is complete. 'Looping' is used to make lines clearer, or to change the nature of the lines altogether, and is a terrific opportunity to clarify/embellish.

In a Steven Seagal film, ADR is often used to help audiences better understand the sheer ferocity of Seagal's blows: e.g. 'Son of a bitch broke my jaw'; 'I've never been hit so hard in my life'; or 'Good God, that handsome man is powerful.'

It's a technique that would have eradicated an unhelpful ambiguity in the otherwise excellent erotic thriller, *Body of Evidence*.

Hot-shot lawyer Frank Dulaney (Willem Dafoe) has begun a torrid sadomasochistic affair with his client, Rebecca Carlson (Madonna), whose potent congress allegedly killed her late lover.* During Dulaney and Carlson's first sexual encounter, she restrains him with his own belt and pours hot candle wax on his chest, stomach and, we are led to infer, his genitals. But we do not get a close-up of Dafoe's engorged tip or sack, meaning the wax could have missed; his anguished facial expression could be a delayed reaction to the still-scalding wax on his nips.

---

* The film's tagline: 'This is the murder weapon. Her name is Rebecca.' But wouldn't the same go for Barry the Strangler? – *Ayo*.

Director Uli Idel would have been wise to insist Dafoe add a line of explanation, the audio of which could have played over a shot of Madonna's face: e.g. 'Watch out! That hot wax is perilously close to my balls!'

As it stands, the confusion bounces me out of the narrative, completely killing my boner.

See: HOT WAX ON BALLS

# AESTHETIC

In the opening shot of Rowdy Herrington's 1989 magnum opus about the secret world of security guards, the camera frames a pair of high heels pivoting out of a recently opened car door, before panning up to a HOT GIRL walking toward a club in a CLINGY DRESS. The title comes up, salmon pink: *Road House.*

Straight off the bat we know this film has *style.*

The title of this chapter is a fancy word for it.

Movies need an AESTHETIC. Why do you think James Bond is so popular? I distrust Foreign Nationals and women as much as the next intimacy-shy sociopath, but these films have much more to offer than the admittedly soothing balm of xenophobia and casual misogyny.

The reason Bond movies give everyone a BONER THAT WON'T SQUASH BACK is simple: they shit style.

Dinner jackets, cufflinks, crisp white shirts, slinky dresses, orchestral swells, après-ski, thin guns, chalets, cars that only seat one passenger – Jesus, it's so sophisticated I'm getting a semi.

Is *your* movie giving the audience a semi?

See: BONERS, UNSQUASHABLE; CLINGY DRESSES; FOREIGN

# ALCHEMY

Danny DeVito on his own is goddam magnificent. Schwarzenegger solo ain't too shabby. But put them together and what you got?

The filmmakers called it *Twins*.

I call it ALCHEMY.

Because although base materials can't turn into gold, high *concepts* can.

See: *WHITE CHICKS*

# ANSWERING QUESTIONS WITH A QUESTION

Like Jesus, the wise protagonist ANSWERS A QUESTION WITH A QUESTION. In Paco Cabezas's 2014 house invasion dramedy *Tokarev*, Paul Maguire (Nicolas Cage), an ex-career criminal tracking down the killer of his teenage daughter, enlists the support of former associates Danny Doherty (Michael McGrady) and Kane (Max Ryan), a man without a surname.

When Doherty asks Maguire, 'How deep do you want to go?' Maguire responds with an inquiry of his own:

'How deep is hell?'

When Doherty, flummoxed, fails to respond, Maguire doesn't follow up the inquiry by saying, 'Seriously, I know it's meant to be hot and all, but how deep do you think it is?' Because Maguire doesn't care how deep hell is. Maguire rejects parameters of any kind: height, breadth, volume – they're all meaningless to him.

Do you think Maguire gives a solitary shit about the distance between the top of something and its bottom?

This is mid-period Nicolas Cage.

Check his jet-black hair. It looks like it's been sprayed from a can. It's a completely different color from anything that exists in the natural world. It's darker than space. His chest hair is *white*. He looks like a kabuki panda. Do you think this man is going to answer any of your *questions*? A question about *dimension*? He don't got time for geometry.

He's only got time for one thing: AN ASS-KICKING RAMPAGE.

See: ASS-KICKING RAMPAGE, AVOIDING SETTING PRE-EMPTIVE PARAMETERS FOR; HELL DEPTHS, DIFFICULTY OF ACCURATELY MEASURING

# ASS

High-end philosopher Plato (dead, Greek) thought that everything on earth was an imperfect copy of its 'ideal form'.

'What is a bicycle pump?' Plato would have said. 'Not the imperfect one I'm pointlessly pummeling – this is but a shadow. Nay, in some other dimension there exists an *absolute* bicycle pump, where its pumpiness is at its most bicycley. And when we picture a bicycle pump, it's this perfect pump of memory that we do behold.'

But a philosophy of pumps won't get us any further down the freeway than a piece-of-shit bicycle.

So what about Man? What is *our* Platonic form? What is our essential *nature*? Where might we find our *soul*?

The Movies, more than 200 years later, have an answer:

In our ASS.

During the climactic showdown of Rowdy Herrington's transcendent 1989 doorman dramedy *Road House*,* local business magnate Brad Wesley (Ben Gazzara) taunts Dalton (Patrick Swayze): 'I see you've found my trophy room, Dalton. The only

---

* I agree with Gordy on this one: the Christ parallels in *Road House* are far richer than those in Spielberg's vastly overrated *E.T.*, which is just an upmarket feature-length episode of *Fraggle Rock – Ayo.*

thing missing is your ass.' Why does Wesley want Dalton's ass so bad?*

We instinctively understand Dalton's ass to be something important, and yet we know that this particular ass – like all ass – does not exist in its own right. Dalton's ass is not something *separate* from the rest of Dalton; it is not a severable *component*. Dalton cannot *hand over* his ass.** Dalton handing his ass to Wesley would be the same as giving Wesley his *essence*. Dalton's ass is Dalton at his *most distilled*. To take Dalton's ass is to take Dalton *himself*.

Because Dalton *is* ass.

And this kind of ass is something far bigger than the 'arses' I grew up with in Glasgow (and that's saying something). Cos an 'arse' is just a coupla cheeks and a syphon system.

So while it's possible to act like an 'arse', to be an 'arse' or even to select a gear for your 'arse' to be in, there's something shrunken about the term, which corresponds to the provincial nature of UK cinema in general.

British Arse lacks the life-affirming expansiveness of American Ass.

That kind of ass – *American Movie Ass* – is made of groin, guts *and* anus. It's so much bigger than an 'arse'. It's the site of our true selves.

---

* I mean – duh – have you seen Patrick Swayze's ass in *Road House*? Plato would've been on that thing like it was the last dinghy left – *Ayo*.
** Although it seems that you can have your ass 'handed to you'. Maybe Ass Exchange is a one-way street? – *Ayo*.

Where 'we' are most 'us'.

Ass.

See: AMERICAN ASS, THE LIFE-AFFIRMING
EXPANSIVENESS OF

## ASS VS HEAD

The enemy of ASS is the HEAD.

The head as represented by The Front Office, The Court House, The Big House and The Country House, all tied up with a Fuck-Off Big Bow of Red Tape.

The head that tries to 'be considerate of other people's feelings' rather than telling it how it is. The head that 'plans' and 'remembers birthdays'. The head that tries to civilize the ass, to make it soft.

But no one wants a soft ass.

We want an ass like a boulder.

Because if you get your ass right, you don't *need* a head. Frankly, the head is just a fancy funnel.

The HEART is the ass's defense against the head. When we listen to our heart, it feels right in our ass. When we *ignore* our heart and listen to our head, we lose our ass for ever.

And a man without an ass is no man at all. Look at Ronnie Wood.

Arnie, Sly, Lundgren: their heads are actually quite unpleasant, like putty gone soft in the heat. But no one's looking at their *heads* . . . you're paying to see their rocking bods and beefy bots.

Movie heroes endure because of their *asses*, not their heads.

See: BEEFY BOTS; HEART, THE; RED TAPE, FUCK-OFF BIG BOW OF; SOFT ASS, UNDESIRABILITY OF

## ASS, FEELING IT IN THE

People talk about their gut. I talk about my ass.

If I know something's right, if something's *really* right, I'll FEEL IT IN MY ASS. I've come to rely on my ass. I know my ass and my ass knows me. My ass won't take any shit from me, and I sure as hell won't take any shit from my ass.

No one in this Town ever came up with a decent pitch using their head.

That thing came out their ass.

See: ASS, RELYING ON YOUR; ASS TALK; GUT TALK; KNOWING YOUR ASS; WRITING FROM YOUR ASS

## ASS, GETTING OFF YOUR

The worst spot a movie character can be in is the same place I spent my entire twenties . . .

On my ass.*

Being on your ass is a fact of life. As soon as Love's Open Throat is squeezed tight by Jealousy's Fist, you can forward any remaining post to: Gordy LaSure, His Ass, Bumsville. It's understandable. It's relatable. It's the Building Block of Narrative.

Act I: In which our HERO gets off his ass.

Act II: In which our hero gets knocked on his ass.

Act III: In which our hero gets back off his ass (and kicks some ass).

That's why the United States has always been wary of a welfare system that functions. It'd be like providing a permanent parking space for ass. I've found that the only way to GET OFF YOUR ASS is to look for a new piece.

In Bruno Barreto's 2003 cabin-crew dramedy *View from the Top*, Donna Jensen (Gwyneth Paltrow) dreams of being a flight

* I pleaded with him. I said that the sentence construction makes it sound like 'the worst place a movie character could be is on *your* [Gordy's] ass'. I said, 'I'll even overlook your inelegant use of prepositions.' He said that he didn't believe in prepositions but, two or three months before, he did have a funny feeling about Michael Jackson – *Ayo.*

attendant. This chick wants to get as far off her ass as it's possible to get within the earth's atmospheric system. This is the kind of gal we can spend eighty-seven minutes with (incl. bloopers and credits).

The hero's struggle is to keep off his ass for as long as possible. That's why every Aaron Sorkin hero walks fast along corridors, while people holding clipboards try to keep up with him. They're literally trying to outrun their own asses. And Sorkin knows that a rolling ass gathers no moss. Heroes power-slide under rapidly dropping portcullises, punch Foreign Nationals, shoot at people for whom we have no narrative empathy and make sweet love to women of above-average attractiveness. Try doing any of these things while keeping your ass still. You kinda can, but no one will thank you. If your characters stay on their asses, the audience will get off *theirs* and haul them outta the theater.

The audience *must stay on their* asses or you'll be broke-ass. So, in many ways, moviemaking is about ass management. A good producer is constantly *positioning* ass, *selecting* the right kind of ass on, behind and in front of the screen, while at all times trying to cover his own.

See: ASS, HAULING; ASS, MANAGING; ASS, OUTRUNNING; ASS, POSITIONING; ASS, SELECTING; EMPATHY, WITHHOLDING; HERO, THE

## ASS, INCURSIONS IN THE

One of the most frequent threats made in cinema is that of an unwanted INCURSION IN THE ASS.

In Félix Enríquez Alcalá's 1997 eco-thriller *Fire Down Below*, Jack Taggart (Steven Seagal) addresses an adversary:

> 'How do you wanna do this? . . . Do you wanna play this game all the way? . . . I'll have three hundred agents come up here in this hick town and crawl up every orifice you got . . . When it's over you can go to your favorite proctologist and get a nice soothing ointment for the hole that hurts the most . . .'

Now, there is no way you could fit three hundred (presumably full-height) men into anyone's ass! The mass to ass ratio is completely wrong! I find anything more than a finger tough going, and if you weren't expecting it, your head's going through the sunroof!

You might argue that Taggart's use of the word 'orifice' means his threat encompasses all bodily openings. But I doubt he's suggesting a bunch of Feds are gonna crawl into the guy's nostrils, ear canals or lacrimal sacs! Taggart is clearly implying the anus.* Have you tried to get a proctologist to treat a damaged lacrimal sac? Trust me, you won't try a second time! Especially if you're both on mescaline!

---

* Or urinary meatus? – *Ayo*.

So why is ass incursion such a go-to threat in action cinema?

Perhaps because, as discussed earlier, the action hero *is* ass. To enter his ass is to enter his soul. His ass is his Achilles heel. It's the site of his ultimate vulnerability. To cross the threshold of his ass means absolute destruction and not, like it would for most of us, a bit of fun (if done with adequate prep/lube).

In George Lucas's vastly overrated 1977 sci-fi exploration of his daddy issues, *Star Wars*, the chief antagonist is an enormous space station called the Death Star. But if you look at it, it's really just a giant jet-black ass, complete with perfectly molded sphincter.

Can I be the first theorist to claim that the climactic attack on the Death Star by Luke Skywalker (Mark Hamill) and the Rebel Alliance (various) represents the Male Caucasian Fantasy of descending into forbidden, exotic ass under cover of night with a group of buddies, having the ride of your life, and then destroying the evidence by blowing up the neighborhood?

See: ASS, VARIOUS

## ASS, KICKING

In the climactic firefight of Joseph Zito's 1988 gut-punch, *Red Scorpion*, Dewey Ferguson (M. Emmet Walsh) is fighting to disable the pinko threat in Africa alongside elite soldier Nikolai Petrovitch Rachenko (Dolph Lundgren). As the combat nears its thrilling climax, Ferguson shouts to Rachenko from the driver's seat of his jeep:

'Keep going, man. Keep kicking that ass.'

This could serve as an epitaph for cinema itself. Movie moments like this teach us how to live.

Because that's all you can do. You've got to locate hostile ass and forcefully set about it with your foot.

What other option do we have?

Talking?!

See: WORDS, WHY USE

## ASS-KICKING, CONCERTED

CONCERTED ASS-KICKING represents the protagonist in his most profound and concentrated 'flow' state.

Foreign Nationals shriek incomprehensibly, women cower in clingy dresses, but the HERO is centered, handing out death like lollipops.

The capture of a weaker colleague/woman/child is probably one of the few things that can stop him, but only for a moment, for once begun, the concerted ass-kick must reach its conclusion: the bloody destruction of all characters from whom the narrative has withheld empathy.

See: HANDING OUT DIFFERENT THINGS, VARYING DIFFICULTY OF; HERO, THE

# AUDIENCE

People say a movie should never look down on the AUDI-ENCE. But what is the audience doing when it's sat on its ASS in a theater?

Lookin' up.

Why?

Because you gotta look up to *something* . . . How can we look up to anyone in Real Life? Everyone in Real Life has betrayed us!

(Also, a movie doesn't have eyes! It's not looking at us at all! And why the hell are these 'people' telling movies where they can look? I'd like to meet some of these 'people' and tell THEM where to look!)

You know the drill by now:* it's the Act III climax and two(+) wealthy actors in body armor are pretending to fight above a cityscape. And while these strangely weightless, make-up-caked behemoths lay waste to the municipal infrastructure, committing countless civil violations as they physicalize their psychodramas, the camera will periodically glimpse a dusting of poorly paid extras gazing skyward, buffeted by carcinogenic movie wind.

---

* Incidentally, this was the tagline to an excellent horror film set in the world of dentistry. I forget the name. *The Scary Dentist*? – *Ayo.*

Why aren't these gormless stacks of fuck ducking for cover? What's wrong with them? Who *are* these people?

I'll tell you who they are. I'll tell you who they *represent* . . .

US!

The movie-going public! WE'RE the saps funding these spandexed fuckers' fortified mansions. WE'RE the ones filling their juicers with superfoods, while THEY make sweet love to this season's swimsuit models! WE'RE the ones powering their decaf mochaccino fountains!

And do you know what would happen if we were to approach one of these colossal turds in a parking lot? They'd vomit on us. And while we were scraping their spew off our flak jackets, they'd signal to one of their security team and we'd be pinned against our jeep before we had time to retrieve a résumé from our camo pants. And when we started to snot-cry, they'd be all like, 'Oh shit. Sorry, we thought you were reaching for a weapon.' And we'd be like, 'Sure – by coincidence there *is* a weapon in our pocket, but we weren't *reaching* for it! We were just taking it out of our pocket first in order to gain easier access to our résumé!'

For a movie to be successful, it *must* look down on the audience.

See: ASS; PEOPLE

# AWARDS

At each AWARDS ceremony people are nominated, or 'nom'd', for various awards. Not all of them will be 'winners'.* In general, only 20 per cent of those nominated go on to win.

That's an 80 per cent failure rate.

And those failures attend these award ceremonies, hubristically ignorant of their inadequacy, nestled alongside their betters as if nothing's fundamentally wrong with them. As if they're not 'worse' than anyone else! In fact, they often look cheery and full of expectation! These losers think there's a chance they might be winners!

There *are* people who know the identities of these losers from the get-go: the members of the judging panels, a shadowy cabal of women devoted to marginalizing men and keeping the film industry a 'chicks-only' zone.

But before you can decry the injustice, the award ceremony starts, and these dames start doling out gongs one by one like little doggy biscuits – it's an insult to art/biscuits!

Results should not be revealed in this manner!

Many of us in the movie business are tightly wound, given to

* People in such a state of triumph that the word describing them will not bear contraction – *Ayo*.

paranoia, with a tendency to lash out when stressed. The whole set-up is divisive!

Here's an analogy: say you begin to experience episodic skin irritation about seven centimeters from your anus, so you go to your local clinic to check it out. They take a swab – it's uncomfortable – the area's red and angry – they send it off for analysis – a couple of weeks elapse – no news – you're in hell – but just as you're about to take out your anger on someone less important, they give you a call to come back to the clinic because they have 'some news concerning the test results', so you go back to the clinic.

When you arrive, what they DON'T DO is then line up four other dudes who have skin irritation seven centimeters away from THEIR anuses and announce which one of you requires surgical intervention.*

So where do these jacked-up 'awards panels' get off? Why do they feel they can torture hard-working, underappreciated movie stars?

What did us artists ever do except try to tell heartfelt stories from an independent perspective, backed by well-thought-out media campaigns before the cut-off for competition entry?

Why do they hold filmmakers in such UTTER contempt?

Well, I've found out.

They're worried that if they told everyone who had won in advance, only the people who had won would show up.

* Could poss. be a good reality show, though – e.g. *Fingers Crossed* with Dr Raj Persaud? – *Ayo.*

These people don't know actors. They don't know actors at all!

Actors show up whether they're invited or not! To anything! You don't need to *entice them*! They just like being *out*.

FYI, AND TO FINISH: A GLOSSARY OF TERMS

The First Award of the Night = Least Important Award

Technical Award = Who Cares

Most Promising Newcomer = A Person Whose Monetary Value Has Yet to Be Established

Best Supporting Actor = A Gendered Award for Someone Not Trusted to Carry a Whole Film

Best Supporting Actress = Any Woman Who Isn't Jennifer Lawrence[*]

Best Documentary Award = A Prize for Films That You Know Are Going to Be Really Good, but for Some Reason the Thought of Watching Them Makes You Tired

Best Screenplay = We Don't Have the Balls to Give the Best Picture Award to This Film

Best Actor = The Best Pretending of the Year by a Male

Best Actress Award = The Best Pretending of the Year by a Non-Male

---

[*] Let's see how well this 'observation' dates – *Ayo*.

## AWARDS HOST, THE

Wherever there is a host there are parasites.

These are the award nominees.

Parasites are dependent on the host for nourishment. This explains why they are so willing to laugh at jokes made at their expense. It also explains why Billy Crystal needs to cover himself in natural yogurt after every speaking engagement.

The AWARDS HOST's jokes may seem edgy, but no more so than being sarcastic to someone while giving them a handjob.

Being famous enough to serve as a punchline is one of the few remaining barometers of approbation left in this sorry business called show.

See: APPROBATION, THE FEW REMAINING BAROMETERS OF; MANUAL STIMULATION, SARCASM DURING

# B

*'These are the moments from which
boners are made . . .'*

# BACKSTORIES

In the 1988 thriller *Above the Law*, 'Nico' Toscani (Steven Seagal) is a Chicago police detective who was forced out of the CIA because he stood up to a scumbag who tortured prisoners in 'Nam.

In the 1990 action thriller *Hard to Kill*, Mason Storm (Steven Seagal) is a Los Angeles police detective who was put into a coma by scumbag policemen who killed his wife when he stood up to corruption.

In the 1990 action thriller *Marked for Death*, John Hatcher (Steven Seagal) is a Chicago police detective who is forced to leave the department because he stood up to scumbag drug dealers who killed his partner, Chico.

Three completely different BACKSTORIES. Three completely different launch pads into explosive action.

Backstories tell you what kind of man you're dealing with. In each of these films you're dealing with a wholly different type of Steven Seagal: a Chicago detective, an LA detective and a Chicago DEA agent. But there's one common thread: payback. Drama is about consequences. And one of the most dramatic things you could ever do is to fuck with Steven Seagal. Because he will not stop until a fearful reckoning is visited upon you. And you can try to take Seagal out of the theaters, but he'll keep coming for you. On video. On DVD. On VOD.

Shit, before long he'll perform live in your house. He. Will.
Not. Stop.

See: SCUMBAGS, VARIOUS

# BADASSERY

*Being* a BADASS is different to *having* a bad ass, e.g. diarrhea and/or persistent IBS.

IBS, or Irritable Bowel Syndrome, is a common condition of the digestive system. Symptoms include cramps, savage gas, the squits and tunnel blocks. Taking a load off can help, but it's no guarantee, let alone a picnic. And I (for one) cannot be touched, approached or in any way looked at during sluicing. I don't care who was 'first', YOU need to leave the bathroom.

Because when I'm in the throes of a full or partial evac, I'm like Lon Chaney in *Wolf Man*: my hairs stand on end, my tongue bulges and I can't go near spring onions.

It just so happens that the Wolf Man is also a badass.

The badass plows his own furrow. A bad ass fouls its own furrow.

See: FOULING FURROWS

# BARE HANDS

The true weapon of the HERO.

In Rowdy Herrington's 1989 doorman dramedy *Road House*, James Dalton (Patrick Swayze) uses his BARE HANDS to rip out the throat of chief henchman Jimmy (Marshall Teague). But importantly for his RELATABILITY, he only resorts to this after a prolonged MAN-ON-MAN FIGHT, culminating in Jimmy's COWARDLY PISTOL-PULL.

Initially, the LOVE INTEREST may be repelled by the sight of a man using his bare hands to perform a THREE-FINGER THROAT-RIP KILL, especially if she hasn't seen the action performed in context.

Case in point: Dalton's lover, Doc (Kelly Lynch), does not know that Jimmy's boss, Brad Wesley (a tired-looking Ben Gazzara), has made a PHONE THREAT to kill either her or Dalton's mentor, Wade Garrett (Sam Elliot), and she certainly didn't see Jimmy pull a piece on Dalton while making a DEATH THREAT AUDIBLE ONLY TO THE PROTAGONIST. So Doc, coming late to the party, forms a double 'X' chromosomal kangaroo court and bangs the gavel down before Dalton has a chance to lodge an appeal.

Women.

Later, in a ONE-TO-ONE FINAL BOSS-CONFRONTATION SCENE, Dalton successfully disarms Brad Wesley (who had foolishly embarked on a LONG PRE-TRIGGER-PULL GLOAT) with a SWEET KARATE KICK. Dalton's hand contorts into the same three-finger throat-rip position, but after A BIG-DECISION STARE into the eyes of a thoroughly exhausted-looking Ben Gazzara (drifting in and out of character, perhaps wondering how he can wisely invest the money from his appearance in *Road House*), he relents, turning to the forgiving eyes of Doc, late to the party once more.

Ever the opportunist, Ben Gazzara's dastardly Wesley pulls his gun and makes to shoot Dalton in the back, only to be gunned down by, in turn, Red Webster (Red West), Emmett (Sunshine Parker), Car Dealership Owner (Jon Paul Jones – not the Led Zeppelin bassist) and Frank Tilghman (Kevin Tighe). Thus, Dalton is denied his homicidal catharsis, and as an audience, we will never respect him again. An otherwise excellent film squanders its potential in the last act.

Result? Mediocre B.O.*

Lesson? Never back down from a KILL OPPORTUNITY.


See: BIG-DECISION STARES; COWARDLY PISTOL-PULLS; DEATH THREATS AUDIBLE ONLY TO THE PROTAGONIST; FIGHT, MAN-ON-MAN; HERO, THE; KILL OPPORTUNITIES, MAKING THE MOST OF; LONG PRE-TRIGGER-PULL GLOATS; LOVE INTEREST, FAILURES OF COMPREHENSION WITHIN THE; ONE-TO-ONE FINAL BOSS

---

* Gordy's gone native, so 'B.O.' means but one thing to him: Box Office. While, to me, BO means Gordy's just wafted into the room – *Ayo.*

CONFRONTATIONS; PHONE THREATS; RELATABILITY;
SWEET KARATE KICKS; THREE-FINGER THROAT-RIP
KILLS

## BARS SUDDENLY GOING SILENT

This only really works just after someone walks into the bar. If the BAR SUDDENLY GOES SILENT for no reason, the audience may become disoriented.

See: *HORACE AND PETE*

# BELIEVABILITY

It is the mid-eighties and two beings from the future materialize in downtown LA.

One is an Austrian ex-bodybuilder programmed to kill the Director's Wife; the other is a man whose face is impossible to remember even while you're looking at it. The Non-Face Guy tells the Director's Wife that she's going to give birth to a child who'll lead a resistance force against an army of machines set on destroying Mankind, which turns out to be one of the best chat-up lines of all time. The Non-Face Guy gets a PITY LAY, but buys the farm later, leaving the Director's Wife to destroy the chief Man Machine in what looks like a massive hydraulic trouser press.

Believable?

The way Jimmy C tells it, you bet. Cameron's 1984 sci-fi meisterstroke, *The Terminator*, taps into something deep within us. We *all* think the human race depends on us. But while it's fun to meet a movie that validates our self-regard, the fact is the machines have already taken over.

Try doing a simple bank transaction with an actual person. It's practically impossible. And when you go into a branch to try and get someone to engage with you, they're gonna have you on file, and they're gonna ask you to leave the building.

*The Terminator* makes us believe our actions count. That they're gonna live on in history. That our kids will amount to something rather than plunder our resources and put on end-of-semester plays denigrating us with their barely veiled caricatures. Do they think we're stupid? That we can't see straight through those cyphers?

But our actions don't count for shit. Except for when we fuck up. Then they count good and long. That's reality.

Care for a dose?

How's about someone you married for about a minute getting half of everything because your lawyer was high on butane when he drafted the pre-nup?

Is that believable?

No. It's fucking *un*believable.

Turns out Misty isn't even her *real name*. It's a 'stage name'. And the reason she travels so much *isn't* because she's fighting for freedom in the Gulf. It's for a completely different and arguably gross reason.

Who wants to believe that their life is actually happening the way it is? Who wants to discover that when they try to brush off that odd dry dust from their hands that, no, that's not dust, that's your skin now, shrunken, yet loose? Who can believe that's *your* face in the mirror, its spotted, powdery flesh concertinaing with each involuntary shrug?

No one.

Because perhaps the only way we can find *any* belief in ourselves is to put what belief we have in *other* people, people who are no longer believable as actual people: film stars.*

And we pay these people unbelievable amounts of money to do unbelievable things in unbelievable circumstances. That's why, when people say they didn't think something was believable in a movie, I lose my lunch. None of it is believable! Brad Pitt is in it! Why isn't every character continually commenting on how handsome he is?!

We don't want BELIEVABILITY. We want the continuation of the *Terminator* franchise.

Folks liked that movie so much they made an unfeeling cyborg state governor!

That's the power of movies: despite bearing no relation to reality, they can seduce millions into making catastrophic choices in their *own* reality.

See: PITY LAY

* And yet, in films, only film stars can 'play themselves' – *Ayo*.

# BETRAYAL

Most dramas, like most marriages, are built on BETRAYAL.

But betrayal is never true betrayal if you are working under-cover. When assuming a fake identity in the fight for justice, the hurt caused by your untruths are, at worst, a 'complication'. The HERO often carries secrets: secrets that no one else can understand, secrets that often come to light only after some fool dame goes and falls in love with him.

As long as the hero meaningfully breaks off relations before returning to his HOMELY WIFE, this falls under the NO HARM, NO FOUL principle – he'll swallow the hurt for all concerned. This 'other' woman tends to maintain fierce loyalty, knowing that the hero is still basically a DECENT MAN and that what they had *was* real.

In John Irvin's 1986 Mafia dramedy *Raw Deal*, Mark Kaminsky (Arnold Schwarzenegger) fakes his own death so he can infiltrate the Mob and track down some lowlifes who iced his buddy's kid. Now operating under the name Joseph P. Brenner, he is practically forced to bone a hot chick called Monique (Kathryn Harrold) for fear of blowing his cover. He never wanted to make sweet love to this woman; it's a mission-specific task that he accomplishes with the kind of masculine majesty that's long since been lost. Today's millennials would probably end up swapping trilbies and playing the ukulele to one another by the charming glow of a window display outside an Olden Time Teddy Bear Emporium, before getting unexpectedly caught in a rain shower.*

But when Joseph P. Brenner completes his mission and becomes Mark Kaminsky once more, he BREAKS THINGS OFF MEANINGFULLY, giving Monique a quarter of a million dollars in stolen drug money so that she can start a new life. She is completely different to the drunk, gambling floozy we met at the beginning of Act II, transformed by the transcendence of physical congress done right.

Similarly, in Félix Enriquez Alcalá's 1997 eco-thriller *Fire Down Below*, local outcast and beekeeper Sarah Kellogg (Marg Helgenberger) feels betrayed by Jack Taggart (Steven Seagal). She thought he was a handyman affiliated to the local church, not a martial-arts-trained Environmental Protection Agent sent to investigate a series of mysterious deaths.

But Taggart assures her that the rapport they've established during the narrative was, and is, real: 'I loved fixing your porch and I'm very interested in you.' She knows this is a man of honor whose only flaw is that sometimes he may be too unwavering in his selfless quest to make the world a better place.

Contrast this with the genuine sense of betrayal expressed when he discovers his boss is covertly working for the same shady company that he's investigating: 'You're a piece of shit and I'm ashamed of you.'

It's rare to see a movie star so willing to express hurt in an open and real way. Perhaps that's why we are forever bound to Seagal.

* And for some reason find it funny! – *Ayo.*

See: BASICALLY DECENT MEN; BREAKING THINGS OFF
MEANINGFULLY WITH FINANCIAL SWEETENERS; HERO,
THE; HOMELY WIVES; UNDERCOVER EXTRAMARITAL SEX,
DE FACTO NO HARM/NO FOUL RULE FOR

# BIOPICS

There's a line in David Lean's punishingly long 1962 desert flick, *Lawrence of Arabia*: 'Truly for some men nothing is written unless they write it.'

Duh.

I don't have a secretary either. I type my *own* pamphlets.

BIOPICS would have you believe that every Great Man got to be 'Great' (so-called) because of their merit. But oftentimes the road forks and you wind up on a bum prong.

It's luck.

Some people have great luck and some people have shit luck – that's all there is to it.

And the people who turn out 'Great' – through *luck*, nothing more – *those* people become the subject of movies that star a bunch of other lucky fucks, who then get awards because they did a 'good' *impression*. And why is their impression so 'good'? Because they were lucky enough to look and sound like the guy in the first place! Look at Benny Kingsley!* He's *lucky* he *already* looked and sounded like Gandhi! Life's a lottery! He got the golden ticket!

People think that a 'Great Guy' *deserved* what he got because

* *Sir* Benny Kingsley . . . – *Ayo.*

– 56 –

of his *character* or his *drive* or his *talent*, and how *amazing* it is that he overcame obstacles and triumphed over adversity, while they *completely ignore* the fact that he was just lucky, lucky, lucky.

There's a butt-load of people who could've been *just* as successful if only the world hadn't taken a giant dump on them for no reason.

Where are their biopics?

There's never going to be a movie about a young screenwriter who had a bad reaction to a bottle of Mai Tai and punched out a sixteen-year-old kid on a golf course – a sixteen-year-old kid who got mad because he found out that this really promising screenwriter had been sort of fooling round with his definitely-over-seventeen twin sister, who then threatened to kill herself (in a pretty unserious way – she hadn't even settled on a *method*) because she found out that there wasn't exactly full disclosure with regard to one of the parties' marital status – a pretty self-righteous sixteen-year-old punk who then turned out to be the beloved only son of the golf course's owner, who happened to be *inappropriately tight* with a development executive at the studio – like, are you going to *develop* or are you going to be the *physical embodiment* of someone else's retributive rage? – and the next thing you know this actually very sweet screenwriter's hot script isn't so hot anymore – in fact, it's cold as old shit – and this really quite thoughtful artist's marriage breaks up because of his then wife's complete refusal to even *try* to understand that this really fairly minor infidelity (barely lasting a summer or so) was nothing more than an *appeal* – a *cry* for the then wife to sit up and take notice that there were maybe some issues that needed (at the very least) to be *addressed* – but there was this complete *resistance* to communicating in *any way whatsoever* – and this unfairly maligned guy – I mean, aren't we *all* responsible for each other at some kind of basic level? – isn't that in the Bible? – are we actually saying there are Good People and Bad People? – is that *really* what we're saying at this point in Human History? – this Christ-like martyr ends up drifting and not using alcohol as a crutch exactly – but more like a buffer – as bubble wrap between his exposed, once-impetuous heart and the acid air – and before he knows it, he starts to see himself as being permanently bubble-wrapped – and he sees himself getting married to these various people – but he's not there – he's just operating this avatar of himself – air goes in and out of his body – but not because he wants to breathe – in fact, he becomes more and more aware of how *involuntary* these breaths are – how greedy and relentless they feel – and that if he could just *decide* to stop – if it were like pressing 'off' on a remote control and he could lie down and not get up again – with no pain – or not too much – just a letting go – like a dimming LED merging into the glassy black of the surrounding glass – he would do that – and although there might be some limited sadness on the part of others – they would be fine – they would most likely *prosper* – so why not lie down for ever?

But they're never going to make that movie! It'd be a total bummer! Even though I know for a fact that all these things happened to a guy I know!

And when this guy who isn't me tells other people, they're *riveted*.

They're like, '*Wow* . . . death . . . heavy . . . Don't die, Gordy. Please. You're not allowed to die. You owe us money.'

Because death can be a powerful tool in storytelling. Many biopics (incl. the interminable *Lawrence of Arabia*) start at the end of their subjects' lives. But be careful not to start too far after, lest you have to account for the time elapsed: e.g. 1980 is an appropriate start for a biopic about John Lennon, but 2280 may seem arbitrary. Or that was the 'note' I got on my script, *Lennon A.D.(e).*, despite the fact that without the framing device of a rusting, Beatles-obsessed cyborg in post-virus Stockport, the whole thing would have no context. Intercutting it with the zombie material was what made it so fresh! See below:*

> We flashback to 1965. John Lennon is trying
> to carry four mugs of tea: three for the
> other Beatles and one for himself. But he's
> overfilled them! Tea starts to spill onto
> his suede Cuban heels (which stain very
> easily). He calls out . . .

>                     JOHN
> Help!

> We see his three band mates exchanging
> glances. Their looks seem to say, 'Perhaps
> our musical colleague needs somebody,'
> though they don't say it out loud for
> reasons of copyright.

>                     JOHN
> Help!

* Gordy insisted on including this extract from his rejected script, hoping to reignite interest in the project – *Ayo.*

*A very old studio technician struggles toward him with noticeably shaky hands.*

*Lennon's eyes seem to qualify the initial exhortation, suggesting that this extremely old/fragile person is not going to be able to provide the assistance he so desperately needs. The band see John's modifying glance, causing a lyric that cannot be printed for legal reasons to pop into their respective moptops.*

*Top shot: the four mugs of tea tumble to the ground.*

*Cut to: the four Beatles in the studio cutting the track 'Help!'. Scouse smiles all round.*

*Dolly in on George Martin, looking like an off-duty BA pilot. He's nodding along with the wry smile of someone who knows how to land a plane in any weather conditions. We cut to George, Paul and Ringo listening to playback. John comes in once more with four teas.*

                    JOHN
Lads - help! I know we just got a fab song
off the back of your previous lack of
response, but this time I mean it. I don't

want to smash yet more mugs. I need a little help from my friends!

*The band exchange looks.*

*Cut to: low-angle shot. Four mugs smash on the ground, one after the other.*

*John and George are in the mixing booth, listening to Ringo sing the last note of 'With a Little Help from My Friends'. George turns to John.*

GEORGE

You see, John Lennon, if we had helped you out with carrying those four overfilled mugs like you'd requested, Ringo Starr would never have had the opportunity to struggle with that long high note at the end.

JOHN

I guess you're right, George Harrison. It's like when I told Mick Jagger to get off that cloud. My sole motivation was to prevent an accident! It was such an unsafe surface for standing . . . I know the guy's light, but even so! Little did I know it would propel them to the toppermost of the poppermost. Which reminds me, where's Paul McCartney, the Beatles' bass player, got to?

                    GEORGE

He's with his current girlfriend, the
aspiring actress Jane Asher.


                     JOHN

The red-headed woman who later goes into
business, specializing in cakes?


                    GEORGE

That's right. She and Paul are trying to
attain mutual satisfaction.


                     JOHN

Are you talking about the Rolling Stones
again, George Harrison?


                    GEORGE

Not in this instance. I'm talking about
how Paul McCartney and Jane Asher are right
this moment trying to achieve simultaneous
orgasm.


                     JOHN

So, in other words, you're saying that
they're trying to –


    *Cut to: boiling kettle.*


                     JOHN

Excuse me, George Harrison. That's the
distinctive whistle of a kettle.


                    – 62 –

*John Lennon stands by a boiling kettle. He
picks it up to pour himself a lovely cup of
Abbey Road tea.*

JOHN
(*to himself*)
Why does George Harrison think I'd care
whether Paul McCartney and Jane Asher come
together?

*Close-up: boiling kettle water cascades to
the floor, soaking John Lennon's Carnaby
Street moccasins.*

*We dolly into John Lennon's face – he's had
another song idea! Then a sudden change of
expression.*

*Close-up of the steaming moccasins. We hear
a scream.*

*John Lennon is on a hospital gurney. A
large-breasted woman wheels him into a
white room.*

JOHN
Look, nurse, my foot will eventually heal!
I only need it for tapping in time. I must
urgently return to my Beatles colleagues –
I've got an idea for a song! I need to get
back!!

*The words 'GET BACK' start to repeat,*
*echoing. The image starts to flash with*
*bright lights.*

*We cut to Paul McCartney, in bed with Jane*
*Asher. He stops mid-pump.*

> JANE ASHER

What do you think you're doing, Paul
McCartney? I'm not even close. Not by a long
shot, if you don't mind.

> PAUL McCARTNEY

I have my reasons, Jane Asher. That was a
psychic message from John Lennon, and I need
to get to one of my musical instruments
ASAP. The only problem is that I left my
favorite bass at Moscow airport – which is a
real drag because I can always rely on it to
inspire me melodically!

> JANE ASHER

You finish what you started, Paul McCartney.
We made a deal, in case you forgot.

> PAUL McCARTNEY

Fair enough, but let's not muck about.

*Macca and Asher recommence lovemaking.*

                    JANE ASHER

I can't believe you left your bloomin'
bass guitar in Moscow. That's back in the
U.S.S.R.!


                  PAUL McCARTNEY

OH, DARLING!


                    JANE ASHER

Did you just climax? Because so did I!


    *Off their look, a montage of the Beatles*
    *recording 'Come Together', 'Get Back',*
    *'Oh! Darling' and 'Back in the U.S.S.R.',*
    *intercut with savage assaults from the*
    *roaming, rotting undead.*


Dynamite, right? And they threw it all back in my face over
what was barely a slap.

See: WOW, BEING LIKE

# BRAWN

Just because a HERO has BRAWN don't mean he ain't got brains to spare. In Rowdy Herrington's 1989 bar-security dramedy *Road House*, Dalton (Patrick Swayze) is a professional 'cooler': an expert doorman able to handle the rowdiest clubs and make them safe for chicks in CLINGY DRESSES.*

But when a cowardly lowlife shanks him in the abs, forcing Dalton to go to Outpatients, we find out he has a degree in philosophy from NYU. The attending physician, Doc (Kelly Lynch), who'll look hot later when she takes off those damn glasses and stops acting like such a tight-ass, tries to hide her surprise:

                         DOC
    Any particular discipline?


                       DALTON
    No. Not really. Man's search for faith. That
    sort of shit.


                         DOC
    How's a guy like you end up a bouncer?**

---

* I've allowed the repetition of plot summations, presuming that those capable of reading this book in sequence are inured to tedium – *Ayo*.
** Perhaps Dalton dropped out of NYU when he realised he'd mistakenly enrolled on the theology course? – *Ayo*.

Just lucky, I guess.

One thing's sure as shit: Dalton will be giving this dame his secret meat by the Act II mid-point.

Sure, he looks like Zeus descended from downtown Olympus's exclusive salon district, but it's Dalton's subtle use of psychology that seals the deal.

Even though he was meaningfully engaged in unlocking the code to the universe, he's not going to bring that shit up unless directly prompted by a SMOKIN' SEÑORITA. He ain't some pencil-neck tuggin' it at his laptop while the other hand double-clicks. He knows brain has its place: second in line to your ASS.

College don't teach you to have a body that broads just want to lose themselves in. You get that rock-hard bod on the streets, busting heads and pounding ass. Fuck his mouth, his torso does the talking!

Any other kind of diploma don't mean diddly.

See: ASS; CLINGY DRESSES; DIPLOMAS, NON-DIDDLY;
HERO, THE; SEÑORITAS, SMOKIN'

# BRITISH CINEMA

François Truffaut said BRITISH CINEMA was a 'contradiction in terms'. But what the hell did he know? The guy died before *Rancid Aluminium* was even *written*.

Lesson? Speak too soon, look like an ass jacket.

Here's another Q in search of an A:

Q: Why do we feel so insanely tired at the merest mention of a British film?

A: Because British films seem to think they should show what life is like to live, whereas good films (cf. the works of Steven Seagal) show you the life you'd *like*:

- being rewarded for mistrusting authority;
- wearing a ponytail without anyone giving you shit;
- using kung fu to deliver on-the-spot corrective justice.

Faced with the prospect of watching some British film about unattractive people in inadequate housing, your body automatically shuts down to protect itself.

On the rare occasions when a female student of mine suggests we watch a British film, I'm crippled with fatigue. How will we find one that's still on? How will we sit through it? How will I cope with the overwhelming feelings of sadness that someone bothered making it?

# I. Can't. Do. It.

See: THE COMPLETE WORKS OF STEVEN SEAGAL
Don't see: BRITISH FILMS

# BURNT-OUT HOMES

Going back to your HOME and finding it BURNT OUT is a bummer, but the true HERO will be quick to seize what is actually an opportunity to go back out into the world and KICK ASS with particular, though not exclusive, emphasis on those ASSHOLES who burnt out said home in the first place which, as well as having cash value, may also have emotional value, even if the home is essentially a modest home.

As the hero looks at his burnt-out home, he will also be able to avail himself of A PRIVATE CRY and/or an audience-empathy-building WHY ME WAIL.

At this point, the score swells, the sky darkens, the wind rises, and our hero is left silhouetted against a hungry wall of fire.

Next scene, this guy's got ASS-KICKING on his mind.

These are the moments from which boners are made.

Fact is, at the start of any flick that's worth a damn, the hero is AN UNOPENED CONTAINER OF ASS-KICKING. The job of a movie's first ten minutes is to locate the ring pull.

See: ASS-KICKING, EFFECTIVE TRANSITIONING FROM CLOSED CONTAINER TO OPEN CONTAINER OF; ASS-KICKING GLOBALLY; ASSHOLES; PRIVATE CRIES; WHY ME WAILS

*'In life, people don't change . . .'*

# CALL TO ACTION

Joseph Campbell, the famous mythologist and soup heir, coined the phrase CALL TO ACTION. It describes the moment in a narrative when the HERO is 'called' to start the adventure. In ancient times, this might be conveyed via a unicorn in a fiery vision, but these days it's often easier to text.

The information delivered in such calls needs to be brief and intriguing. For example:

INT. CRAMPED APARTMENT

Buck lies face down on a single bed. The floor is covered with empty bottles of hooch. A baby rhino has gone to sleep on his back. Rough night. The telephone rings. Buck picks up, still groggy from his whiskey bath.

                    BUCK
(*instead of 'hello'*) I don't know where your
wife is –

                    VOICE
              (*off screen*)
Rico's dead. You're next.

*We hear the click of a cradled receiver,*
*then the dial tone.*

                    BUCK
              (*to the rhino*)
You're gettin' heavy.


                    RHINO
I'll quit eating when you quit drinking.

This is a great scene. It's punchy, and we know we're going to have a crap-load of fun with that rhino.

Now let's imagine a version of this same scene in the hands of a less skilled screenwriter . . .

    INT. CRAMPED APARTMENT

    *Buck lies face down on a single bed. The*
    *floor is covered with empty bottles of*
    *hooch. A baby rhino has gone to sleep*
    *on his back. Rough night. The telephone*
    *rings. Buck picks up, still groggy from the*
    *whiskey bath.*


                    BUCK
    (*instead of 'hello'*) I don't know where your
    wife is –


                    VOICE
              (*off screen*)
    Rico's dead. You're next.

                            BUCK
Sorry, who is this?


                            VOICE
                        (*off screen*)
Excuse me?


                            BUCK
You heard me: to whom am I speaking?


                            VOICE
I'm not really meant to say. My evil
superior just told me to 'sound
threatening'.


                            BUCK
Because what you've just said makes
literally no sense: 'Rico's dead' and then
'I'm next'. What do you mean, 'I'm next'?
Is it, 'Now *you* tell me someone who's dead,'
or is it that *I'm* going to be dead next?
Because the latter's unlikely. In the time
between your telling me Rico's dead and that
I'm next, someone else has probably already
died. That's just the life cycle. So I can
only assume that you're threatening to kill
me. Sorry, I didn't get your name -


                            VOICE
Adrian.

                    BUCK

Right. Adrian. So, *Adrian*, I can only assume
that you're threatening to kill me, which is
*against the law* –


                   ADRIAN

It might not be me personally. It could
be someone else within the organization.
It really depends on scheduling and how
difficult you'd be to kill.


                    BUCK

I want to say that I wouldn't be the hardest
person in the word to kill, but I'd like to
think that I wouldn't be the easiest.


                   ADRIAN

Okay, well, that's helpful. So, assuming
we initially sent some weaker operatives to
kill you and they failed, what we'd do is
send some slightly better ones, and after
they failed, we'd slowly work our way up the
ranks until it reached my evil boss who, at
that quite late stage, would probably insist
on handling it personally. He usually only
gets 'hands-on' toward the end. Until then
he's normally on the phone being sarcastic
or saying, 'How difficult can it be to
kill someone?' And sometimes he'll shoot a
subordinate in the face – like totally out of
*nowhere* – and we'll all gasp and say sorry,

and he'll say, 'I'm tired of your excuses!'
- all shouty. But I have to say I think that
if our evil boss were more involved right
up front rather than retrospectively picking
apart the actions of his subordinates, he
might come across as less erratic. Because
sometimes I'm like - hello - I don't live
in your head - maybe *tell* me how to break
up that rival crime cartel rather than just
expecting me to do it without any guidance
whatsoever and then making me feel shitty
that I couldn't do it when - if you think
about it - I'm still a relatively *new*
criminal - like I haven't committed that
much crime as such - I've been more of a
coordinator - and there's ZERO mentoring.
It's sink or swim, totally - but I'd say
that's how everything's going - society has
become so individualized that -

                    BUCK
Adrian, I'm going to stop you there - the
failings of your organization's management
structure are of limited interest to me -
so I'm just going to give you some bullet
points -


                   ADRIAN
I'm sorry - I'm blurting - I think I keep
this rage bottled up - so when I get a
chance to express myself -

                              BUCK

Adrian. Eyes on the prize. Okay, so - one -
I don't know a Rico; two - this is a private
residence, so you shouldn't be calling so
early -


                            ADRIAN

It's 2 p.m.


                              BUCK

Is it? Wow, that's embarrassing.


                            ADRIAN

I'm sorry, can I just check I have the right
number? I'm looking for a 'Fingers' McClaw?


                              BUCK

No. I'm Buck 'The Hammer' Jackson.


                            ADRIAN

You're kidding. Buck! This is Adrian.


                              BUCK

You said.


                            ADRIAN

'Two-Faced' Adrian!


                              BUCK

Stop it!

ADRIAN

It is! I can't believe it. Do you still have
that baby rhino that sleeps on your back?

BUCK

Sure do! He's sleeping on my back right now!

RHINO

I was, until you two started yacking for
about an hour.

ADRIAN

Still as sassy as ever, I hear!

RHINO

I'm too tired to be sassy.

BUCK

Some of the asides he makes are so cutting.
Honestly, it's as if he has them prepared.
But, and this is the irony, he can't take
it. He gets so hurt if you make any kind of
crack to *him*. I always say –

RHINO AND BUCK

'I thought rhinos were meant to have thick
skin!'

*They all laugh.*

                          BUCK
You sound so different!


                         ADRIAN
Well, the last time we met I was using the
Mexican accent.


                          BUCK
Of course! I remember it being very generic
and lazy.


                         ADRIAN
It was SO generic and SO lazy. It was kind
of racist.


                          BUCK
It WAS kind of racist! Well, this has been
great - we should meet.


                         ADRIAN
I would LOVE to meet. As soon as we're done
with this honor killing we should get dim
sum. There's a great All You Can Eat place
quite close to where we bury our victims.


                          RHINO
We'll be there!


        *They all laugh again.*

Full confession: I started to write this scene as an example of what NOT to do, and ended up LOVING it. So go figure. Movies aren't about rules; they're about creating characters that endure. And those characters can be terse as shit or talkative as tits.

Let's try again. How NOT to do the 'call to adventure'. Here goes . . .

>     INT. SMALL APARTMENT - EVENING
>
>     Connor, a lithe, muscular man in the prime
>     of his life (50s/60s), lies on his back
>     staring straight up, his noble brow filled
>     with dreams, darkness, danger . . . He is
>     naked except for jeans, cowboy boots, gun
>     belt, shirt and trucker hat + body warmer.
>     The room's only sound? The contented, post-
>     multi-orgasmic sighs of his girlfriend,
>     Candy (20s, huge tits), draped greedily
>     over Connor's compact chest. She is
>     completely naked. The phone rings.
>
>                         HARRIS
>     Connor?
>
>                         CONNOR
>     Harris?
>
>                         HARRIS
>     I have a situation.

CONNOR

Have you any idea how *late* it is? It's like
ten o'clock. If I hadn't just had sex, I'd
be in my pyjamas by now.


HARRIS

Connor, I ain't fuckin' with you, we have a
situation.


CONNOR

Well, *I'm* certainly not fucking with *you*,
Harris. It's rude to ring so late. I
could've been asleep. In fact, I was asleep.


CANDY

Who is it?


CONNOR

It's Harris . . .


CANDY

Harris? Has he any idea how late it is? It's
ten already!


CONNOR

I'm trying to tell him! (*to Harris*) Now
you've woken up Candy.


CANDY

Well, I'm going to say my last line in this
scene now: fuck y'all, I'm taking a bubble bath.

CONNOR

Jesus, Harris, Candy's so pissed she's
broken the fourth wall.


HARRIS

I'm sorry, Connor, the last thing I wanted
to do was force Candy into a sudden meta
gesture.


CONNOR

She's always saying, 'Unplug the phone
after eight o'clock.' I say, 'What if it's
an emergency?' She says, 'What emergency
can't wait till the morning?' I say, 'What
if my mom falls in the night?' And she
says, 'She lives overseas – what are we
going to do? Charter a jet in the middle
of the night? There's nothing that can't
wait till morning . . .' You know she's the
very practical type . . . But she's also
physically attractive, which is important –


HARRIS

Connor!


CONNOR

What is your problem, Harris?


HARRIS

I need your help.

CONNOR

Well, spit it out then. My hot young
girlfriend's in a bubble bath aching for my
secret meat.


HARRIS

I can't tell you on the phone.


CONNOR

Oh, this is beautiful. You call me up in the
middle of the night -


HARRIS

It's nine forty-five.


CONNOR

It's near enough ten!


HARRIS

Can we meet to discuss this in person?


CONNOR

Are you going to be on time?


HARRIS

What's that meant to mean?


CONNOR

What do you mean, 'What's that meant to
mean?' It's not a friggin' riddle - it's a
simple question. Are you going to be on time?

                         HARRIS

Of course . . .


                         CONNOR

Because sometimes you're late.


                         HARRIS

I'm rarely late. Look -


                         CONNOR

I would say you're *frequently* late.


                         HARRIS

That's not true.


                         CONNOR

I'd say one out of every three times is
frequent.


                         HARRIS

I'll be on time.


                         CONNOR

Okay. Where?


                         HARRIS

The docks.


                         CONNOR

Oh, not the docks. I hate the docks. We
always meet by the docks and it's SO windy.

And I never know what to wear. Should I
dress docker-y or just normal? Either way,
I stick out. Couldn't we go to that new
breakfast place . . .

                    HARRIS
What I need to say I can't say over
breakfast.

                    CONNOR
I could do a brunch . . .

                    HARRIS
Are you not detecting a tone of urgency in
my voice?

                    CONNOR
What I am detecting is stress. And it seems
to me that you're just dumping your stress
on me.

                    HARRIS
Oh, come on.

                    CONNOR
Which is what you always did, and why I
couldn't be your partner anymore. Why do you
think Chad left? You did exactly the same
thing to him . . .

HARRIS

Chad had emotional problems.


CONNOR

That's right, blame the other person.
It's never you, is it? It could never be
your fault. You could never even be *part*
responsible. I loved being a cop. I loved
the long hours, I loved being accountable
to a team, I loved the paperwork, but what I
could not bear, what I could *never* bear, was
your *stressiness*. So, no, I will not meet
you by the docks.


HARRIS

I'm sorry.


CONNOR

I don't want to hear 'sorry'. I'm not
interested in sorry. I want to see a *change
in behavior*. I want to see an alteration in
*manner*. And when that happens, maybe we can
go on a revenge mission together, but until
then, I'm going to focus on being around
people who want me to be the best me I can
be. Good night.


*Connor slams down the phone. End of scene.*

As you get older, the less you feel the call to do anything. Seeing if you can stay awake once you sit down is an adventure. On the few occasions that my phone does ring (and it's not me calling it to find out where the hell I left it), I look at the thing like it's a French wasp, hoping it won't bite. So although that was another great piece of dialogue that rings as true as Gabriel's Own Bell, it's probably best to keep your call to adventure brief.

Got gas in the tank for one more spin around the block?

Buckle up.

> HARRIS
>
> Connor?

> CONNOR
>
> Harris, you son of a bitch - it's been a while.

> HARRIS
>
> I have a tricky situation.

> CONNOR
>
> What other type is there?

> HARRIS
>
> The type only you can handle. Be at the docks at 7 a.m. tomorrow. I'll find you.

> *Click.*

Rip this last page straight outta the book.

It's ready to shoot.

# CASTING

How do you keep an audience in *The Grip of Film* for ninety minutes or more?

CASTING Steven Seagal is a good start.

Why?

Because if you suspect the filmmakers have made bad decisions, like not casting Steven Seagal, you can't truly give yourself over to the work.

Movies that *don't* star Steven Seagal threaten to break the bond of trust between storyteller and audience.

Casting the right actor is crucial.

If there *isn't* a part for Seagal, maybe you're not done writing yet.

See: NOT CASTING STEVEN SEAGAL, THE INSANITY OF

# CATHARSIS

One of the most cathartic acts in cinema is justifiably killing
someone worse than you.

See: ANY GOOD MOVIE

# CHANGE

Memorable movie characters tend to go through some kind of life-altering event. In Orson Welles's 1941 multimedia mangle *Citizen Kane*, the shame of dropping a snow globe causes an old man to die.

In Bruno Barreto's flight-attendant saga *View from the Top*,* Donna Jensen (Gwyneth Paltrow) changes from a small-town girl with cheaply dyed hair and tackily tight clothes to a commercial pilot with expensively dyed hair and costlier tight clothes. But these are merely circumstantial changes – not enough to convict someone. For the film to work (and it works like hell) it's important that Jensen undergo an internal CHANGE. And I don't mean the menopause (though she does look pretty tired by the end). What she learns is that having a good relationship is almost as important as being successful at work, but make sure you nail the work part first or you'll always be a loser. (Note: w/r/t the American Dream there's no such thing as being unsuccessful in your career and successful in relationships.)

Characters can change even more profoundly than in *Top*. In Russell Mulcahy's 1986 medieval dramedy *Highlander*, a French Man (Christopher Lambert) transcends mortality to

---

* Those interested in a deeper discussion of *Top* can consult my monograph, 'Ayoade on *View from the Top*: A Modern Masterpiece' – *Ayo*.

become both Scottish and a symbol for Ultimate Good, two things that were hitherto a contradiction in terms.

In The Works of Steven Seagal, our titular HERO is *already* a symbol for Ultimate Good. Seagal's movies are really about the journey *other people* must undertake to realize *his* unlimited power, be they feisty yet vulnerable women aching for his touch, or pumped-up pricks who he'll humiliate with his unique brand of slow karate.

In life, people don't change. Wives change. Does this mean that wives aren't people? It's the job of movies to ask these questions. So how come there hasn't been a movie about the fact that wives are probably not people? Well, guess what? You're wrong as shit. They made one. It's called *The Stepford Wives*.

Only flaw?

You can't help but sense the *implication* that the smiling submissiveness of these women is meant to be a bad thing.

See: HERO, THE

# CHARACTER

CHARACTER is action.

If you walk out on me, you're a whore. It doesn't matter whether you 'actually' charged me for sex, it's your *actions* that make you a lowdown whore.

No one is born a killer. You become a killer by your *action* of killing someone. And trust me, it doesn't matter whether you were properly trained to use that machine or not. If someone dies and it was your shift, it's on you. And if you were drunk, put your shit in storage, because you're going to *jail.* Not even being white can get you out of that one.

If character *is* action, and it is, the truest character study is the fight sequence, which makes Jackie Chan the greatest character actor of all time.

# CHARACTER STUDIES

If someone describes a movie as a CHARACTER STUDY, we all know what they mean: 'This thing's gonna be slow as shit.'

If *Rocky* were boring, they would call it a character study.

*Raging Bull* is a character study.

The studio didn't even pony up for color film stock. Fancy humming the theme tune to *Raging Bull*? Didn't think so. If I want to see a fat fuck talk to himself in the mirror, I'll put CCTV in my bathroom.

*Predator* isn't a character study. Is there any moment in time when you're doing something better than watching *Predator*? I'd rather be watching *Predator* now, and I'm having sex with someone.

See: BATHROOM SURVEILLANCE, PROS AND CONS; GOING TO CHARACTER UNIVERSITY AS A MATURE STUDENT

# CHOPPERS

If a fleet of jet-black CHOPPERS ain't cresting over a back-lit hill by the end of Act II, you've got to start asking yourself whether this is a movie or a fucking art installation.

See: MOVIE, IS IT A

## CITIES AS CHARACTERS

They're not. All right? New York is not a 'character' in the movie. Characters DO things. What is New York *doing*? It's just there, sucking the life out of everyone, charging too much rent and getting crazy hot every summer.

Also, your city is too tall.

See: CITIES, IDEAL HEIGHTS FOR

# COSTUME

They say that clothes maketh the man. What they don't tell you is that they can also breaketh him. I once wore sports sandals with drop-crotch trucker pants to a funeral and didn't get a second date for a month.

Clothes can BE a narrative. In John Irvin's 1986 action benchmark *Raw Deal*, former-FBI-agent-now-small-town-sheriff Mark Kaminsky (Arnold Schwarzenegger) tells us his story by *what he wears*.

Let's chart the key outfits chronologically:

## ACT I

### MEET MARK KAMINSKY

Blue jeans, large jeans belt, tucked-in red lumberjack shirt.

### INCITING INCIDENT/COMPLICATION

Blue jeans, jean jacket, large jeans belt, tucked-in blue lumberjack shirt.

Note: the jean jacket could be seen as the physical embodiment of this complication.

## ACT II

### SHIT GETS REAL (IN HIS NEW UNDERCOVER IDENTITY

AS CONVICTED FELON JOSEPH P. BRENNER)

Gray flannel pants w/a crisp open white shirt and blue blazer.

A SETBACK

Tighty whitey T-shirt with piping round the sleeves + neck (which, by the way, really shows off his killer bod – he is busting out of this thing, it can barely contain him).

RECOVERY

Large mid-brown double-breasted jacket, chocolate-brown shirt, champagne tie, dove-gray pants and saddle-brown suede shoes.

MONTAGE SECTION – KAMINSKY BLOWS HIS COVER

A series of chunky double-breasted suits. (Can you imagine being Arnie's tailor? How do you even get a tape around those things?)

## ACT III

SHIT GOES DOWN

Black jeans, white vest, black leather jacket.

THE HERO RETURNS

Blue jeans, large jeans belt, tucked-in blue lumberjack shirt.

So, what do these eight distinct outfits teach us? Suits are for stiffs. Just like any true HERO, Arnie can only be his true self in tight jeans.

Tight jeans can be teamed with:

a white vest

*or*

a white T-shirt

*or*

a lumberjack shirt

+

a jean jacket

*or*

a leather jacket.

That's it.

Deal with it.

See: HERO, THE; IT, DEALING WITH

# COUNTDOWNS

There is no film that could not be improved by regularly cutting to a COUNTDOWN.

What is New Year's Eve except a bunch of people counting backwards? And this event fills every capital city the world over. Annually!

It's so compelling that people feel it's worth televising.

What is a film except a countdown? I don't care how good your movie is, we're all just waiting for it to end.

# COUNTING ON PEOPLE

Everyone you'll meet will let you down. Apart from the HERO. You know who the hero is. He's played by the best-paid actor. He gets top billing. And he's the only man you can trust.

Why?

You keep his colonics flowing. You fund his yacht parties. You pay for him to pay other people to keep people like you away from him.

He *needs* you. That's why he'll keep playing that character you like in every movie you see him in. He'll speak in the same voice and wear the same clothes and brush his hair just the way you like it – you know how it frames his face just right? He'll be the same in the interview about the film as he is in the film. He'll tell funny stories that initially appear to be self-effacing.

He refuses to be a slave to variety.

See: COLONICS, FLOWING; HERO, THE

# CRUELTY

Why is it okay that Steven Seagal breaks the Foreign National's arm by bending it the wrong way at the elbow? Because the Foreign National *deserved* it. He was standing in the way of righteousness. Righteousness, in a Steven Seagal film, is symbolized by Steven Seagal.

Why, when the evil drug baron blows smoke in Steven Seagal's tiny eyes, do we feel it to be so unjust? Because the evil drug baron is blowing smoke into the comically small eyes of righteousness itself.

But were Steven Seagal to blow smoke in the face of the evil drug baron or another OBVIOUS ASSHOLE, esp. an AUTHORITY FIGURE MOUTH-WRITING CHECKS IN EXCESS OF HIS ASS'S PREDETERMINED CREDIT ALLOWANCE, it becomes a gesture of defiance, a celebration of individuality, and a true sign of the HERO.

CRUELTY isn't about what is being done; it is a matter of *who is doing what to whom*. Hence American foreign policy.

The charismatic cop beating up someone because they're withholding information is totally different to some new stepdad trying to make the charismatic cop feel small in front of his daughter by buying her what, on the surface, seems like a more thoughtful gift.

The first instance is okay; the second is worse than genocide.

See: ASSHOLES, OBVIOUS; BAD PEOPLE; CHECKS IN EXCESS
OF [ONE'S] ASS'S PREDETERMINED CREDIT ALLOWANCE,
THE MOUTH-WRITING OF; HERO, THE

# CURSES

A CURSE is anything that *limits* a person, *lowers* them or *blocks* them from their full potentiality.

Impotence is a curse.

Many myths involve a character being changed into an animal, such as a frog. Because being a frog is totally limiting. Sure, it might be nice to hop a little better, but you can't get a restaurant reservation. You can't even get a driver's license!

Being a frog stinks!

Menstruation is often called 'the curse' because it stops women, for 'a period', from even *trying* to be nice.

That's why *Curse of the She-Wolf* never did any business. Who wants to see a lycanthrope blaming everyone else for her problems?

See: RESPONSIBILITY, TRY TAKING SOME

# CUTS

Sometimes you gotta make a CUT. I don't care if you're in the edit bay or a knife fight. A shit-heap of kick-butt movies have* benefited from dumping scenes surplus to requirements.

Did you miss the pole-vaulting tournament in *12 Years a Slave*?

Did you miss the titular street-diarrhea scene in *Inside Out*?

Did you miss the first three episodes of *Star Wars*?

Nah.

Wanna know why?

You never saw them.

And you never needed to.

* Surely 'has'? The 'shit-heap' here is singular. Gordy said 'has' sounded 'fuckin' goofy' and that grammar was for 'ass-handlers' – *Ayo*.

## CUTTING TO THE CHASE

Any good editor will tell you the same thing: CUT TO THE CHASE.

But don't cut *during* the chase.

Ideally, you should cut out all the material between your *various* chases.

Do you remember seeing a chase sequence in Orson Welles's 1941 tycoon tale *Citizen Kane*?

Neither do I.

The most exciting moment in that dud is when the super-old dude at the start drops a snow globe – an incident that really should have been mined for laughs.

If he was so ill, why the hell is his so-called nurse allowing him to hold *glass* souvenirs?

He's well enough to shake it, then the next minute he's dead?

Please.

(Don't) See: *CITIZEN KANE*

# D

*'I don't bake cookies for a living . . .'*

# DAUGHTERS

The modern HERO often has a DAUGHTER. This allows an aging action star to interact with a young female character without the complications of sexual tension. Instead, the love story can be played out with her mother/his ex-wife, who, with sensitive lighting, can be played by an actress in her mid-thirties.

A narrative featuring a daughter also allows the filmmakers to prominently feature HOT ASS on the poster, rather than some rancid old catastrophe.

The daughter's role is simple: to be continually wrong.

*She is worried that her daddy doesn't love her enough . . .*

Wrong. He loves her more than she could ever know. It's just that on several occasions he's needed to save – you know – HUMANITY, plus the mission was classified actually. It's not *his* fault that he's an assassin with an unparalleled skill set who feels ethically compelled to defend his country and the freedom of the West without seeking personal gain.

*She is worried her daddy isn't good enough . . .*

Wrong. Even though he's broke, violent and possibly alcoholic. Those things give him *color.*

And the new stepdad, despite the fact that he's never killed someone by twisting their head quickly, is actually *evil.* Okay, so the new stepdad got the daughter a white Ferrari rather than a second-hand ride-on lawnmower with a big pink bow on it, but he probably got his *secretary* to book One Direction* for his daughter's Sweet Sixteen. And that shit don't mean squat if it don't come from the heart. Because money and status are not cool. Working in asset management is not cool. Wearing a suit and knowing what kind of wine to order is not cool. Being 'sensitive' to other people's needs is not cool.

Busting ASS, smelling musty and being intuitively right in every situation while administering on-the-spot justice is cool.

*She thinks that her friends are cool . . .*

Wrong. Her dad is actually way cooler than them.

*She thinks some silly young punk kid is sexy . . .*

Wrong. Her dad is way sexier. He's actually super-sexy – even her friends tell her so. And yet she cannot possess him carnally. That tragedy is also her freedom. Because of the societal injunction against incest, this impossibly sexy man can finally have a meaningful relationship with a hot woman who *doesn't* want to uncoil his secret length.

*She thinks it's cool to party . . .*

Wrong. It's actually cooler *not* to party. Parties are filled with danger and debauched punk kids trying to get her hooked on reefer.

*She thinks travel broadens the mind and that France is more or less safe . . .*

* Because this reference won't date – *Ayo.*

Wrong. Foreign countries are filled with dangerous anti-American insurgents, hooked on reefer, intent on kidnap.

*But occasionally the daughter can teach her old man a small lesson that he already knows . . .*

In McG's 2014 brain-tumor dramedy *3 Days to Kill*, absent father and CIA agent Ethan Renner (Kevin Costner) has an argument with his daughter after he's rescued her from a DOUCHE-Y GUY AT A PARTY. Angry, he asks her to get on the bike that he inexplicably bought her earlier in the movie. She says she doesn't know how to ride a bike.

At this point, some filmmakers would have allowed the audience to put two and two together. But McG knows that his audience didn't illegally download this film for educational purposes.

ETHAN RENNER
What kind of kid doesn't know how to ride a bike?

ZOOEY RENNER
The kind of kid who never had a father to teach her.

If you think Ethan Renner's going to rest before Zooey Renner knows how to ride that bike, you don't know Ethan Renner. By close of business, Zooey is cycling, for the first time, by the steps of the Sacre Coeur. At first glance, an oddly public place to learn, but it means that she can be applauded by strangers when she finally balances. In commercial cinema, personal breakthroughs don't mean diddly until they're publicly validated by large groups.

Ethan Renner learns that it's never too late to realize how good a father he already is.

See: ASS; ASS, HOT; HERO, THE; HUMANITY; OLDER MEN, INHERENT COOL OF; PARTY, DOUCHE-Y YOUNG GUY AT THE

# DIALOGUE

Should be:

    1. Economical.
    2. See 1.

Two of my favorite lines are (in no particular order):

'Dial, dipshit'

and

'Fuck justice.'

DIALOGUE, by contrast with our shitty lives, must move forward. It can't just drift like a polystyrene crust on a stagnant pond. Let's take an ordinary, everyday scene:

> INT. SOME CHEAP APARTMENT - COULD BE ANY TIME
>
> *Buck (fifties, virile, looks thirties) is talking with Candy (twenties, impossibly hot, with a fiery temper to match; smarter than she looks, but not overly so), who is trying on different outfits.*
>
>              CANDY
> Buck? Bucky baby?

BUCK

If I was asleep, I apologize.


CANDY

Which one do you like?


BUCK

Definitely that one.


CANDY

Which one?


BUCK

The one you're wearing.


CANDY

Well, that's funny, because I'm wearing
something completely different to when you
last said that.


BUCK

I know, I was -


CANDY

Which might *indicate* that I've *changed my
mind* as to what I'd like to wear.


BUCK

That's why -

CANDY

Or that you don't care. Which I think is
more likely. You just don't care.

BUCK

I really do. I care so much about our
getting this outfit right.

CANDY

Oh, so I have to ask your *permission* before
I change?

BUCK

No, of course I -

CANDY

Oh, thank you. Thank you so much for
allowing me to decide what I may or may not
wear.

BUCK
(*justifiably bitter*)
It's just that we're a little late.

CANDY

Fuck you. Don't put that on me. I don't even
want to go out. They're your friends, not my
friends.

BUCK

They're our friends.

CANDY

My friends don't patronize me.


BUCK

Well, let's not go then.


CANDY

We *have* to go, Buck. They're our *friends*.
You don't just cancel whenever it suits you.
That's what animals do.


BUCK

Fine, let's go.


CANDY

I am *already* going. I'm trying to go *now*.


BUCK

Do animals make dinner reservations?


CANDY

But I'd like to *not* be naked. Which means
I have to put *clothes* on. Which means I
need to *choose* some. Unless you just want
me to wear the same thing every day *like a
prisoner.*


BUCK

That's –

CANDY

Why don't you just get me some prison
pyjamas and I'll wear those? Like in the
death camps. Then people might see the hell
I'm in.


BUCK

I also liked the other one you put on.


CANDY

Thanks for the mandate, but it's a little
*late* to be engaging with me now.


BUCK

I'm very engaged with you. Why else would I
have taught you the word 'mandate'?


CANDY

You've never shown interest in anything I
do.


BUCK

How do you mean?


CANDY

Why don't you ask a question once in a
while? Would it kill you to ask a question?


BUCK

Do you think you might be getting closer to
deciding?

                    CANDY

Ask me a question, Buck!


                    BUCK

Didn't I just ask you a question?


                    CANDY

Ask! Ask! Ask!


                    BUCK

Does this count as a question?


                    CANDY

You are killing me! You are *literally*
killing me!


                    BUCK

Could I get a little clarification on how
you're using the words 'question' and
'literally'?


    *Ad infinitum.*


This isn't a dialogue scene. This is what happens before you call
an exorcist.

Candy detests the blameless Buck, and there's nothing he can
do. Nothing will change. There will be no redemption.

Contrast this sorry affair with a bitchin' exchange from Peter
Hyams's 1994 futural procedural *Timecop*.

SOME PERSON
Is this T.E.C.* thing dangerous?


WALKER
I don't bake cookies for a living.


Walker (Jean-Claude Van Damme) doesn't even answer the question; he just mentions one of the many jobs that he hasn't chosen to pursue professionally. He may as well have said, 'I'm not currently on a kayak.' This is a guy who says what he wants, when he wants, whether it makes sense or not.

Let's close up shop with some tips for memorable dialogue:

– *Listen to how people talk.* Don't just tune them out. It's tempting, especially when they start talking about their summers or how this person said this thing to them and how they felt about it, like some in-store listening party for petty grievances.

– *How* do people talk? Do they have funny foreign accents? Write out their dialogue phonetically. Don't worry about being racist!

– Are they capable of reason, or is everything they say a barely veiled attack on you?

– Do they use profanity, or do they just judge *you* for using it?

– Do they stop using profanity around a child because they're

---

\* BTW, if you're wondering what T.E.C. is, it's explained in an earlier briefing scene with commendable economy: 'We have to form a new agency to police this technology and protect time. It will be called the Time Enforcement Commission, or the T.E.C.' – *Ayo.*

under the quaint illusion that a six-year-old has never heard the 'c'-word before?

– Are they deluded? Are they completely blind and deluded in a way that's kind of *frightening*?

– Are they capable of laughing? Like would it *kill* them to sometimes laugh when they *know you're being funny*, or do they just do a tight, ugly, place-holder snort?

– Are her eyes alive? Or are they like matte oval tiles?

– Start to secretly record *everything* she says to you, and then make sure you back up the files. It can be useful for arbitration, or even a script, if that script is about an immature person unable to experience gratitude.

## DRIVING CARS THROUGH WALLS/
## WIRE FENCES/SHOP WINDOWS

Don't be a baby about it, just put your foot to the floor and step outta the rubble before the whole thing blows.

You'll need to kick YET MORE ASS once the Feds catch up.

See: ASS, YET MORE

# DUTY

In movies, as in life, women are always trying to stop men from doing what they need to do.

Men, in response, invoke the language of necessity:

> *'I don't have a choice.'*
>
> *'I have to go.'*
>
> *'The city needs me.'*

He cannot say:

> *'Although both options are open to me, I'd rather risk my life out there than spend another second with you.'*

A woman will not allow you to do *anything* unless you convince her that you are being compelled *against your will.*

The movies reflect this.

See: WOMEN, ALL

*'When the job's done, I walk . . .'*

# EDUCATION

I'll tell you a coupla scenes you'll never see in a Steven Seagal joint:

1. The scene where he goes through a list of his academic qualifications.
2. The scene where he recounts his gap year.

You wanna know where I went to school?

I'll give you a clue.

If you ain't dead, you're in the catchment area.

I'm talking what Cosby oughta get:

LIFE.

It's the only school I ever went to.*

See: LIFE, SCHOOL OF

---

* With the exception of the actual schools he attended – *Ayo*.

# EXPRESSIONS

You can write a pretty decent script by putting the following
EXPRESSIONS in any order you like:

*'Let's smoke these guys.'*
*'That's chump change.'*
*'We need to talk.'*
*'You look like shit.'*
*'Afternoon, gentlemen.'*
*'I have a report to file.'*
*'Ring a bell?'*
*'He was my partner.'*
*'I never quit.'*
*'You're shitting me.'*
*'Who sent you?'*
*'I can live with that.'*
*'I run the show.'*
*'Come on, hotshot.'*
*'I'm outta here.'*
*'When the job's done, I walk.'*
*'Anybody wants to walk, do it now.'*
*'Take the train, buddy.'*
*'Your ass is mine.'*
*'He's got this whole town in his pocket.'*
*'You can leave any time you want to.'*
*'Let me fix it.'*

*'I'll handle it.'*
*'I'll find them.'*
*'Finish him.'*
*'The guy's got a rap sheet as long as my dick.'*

# EYES

If EYES are the windows to the soul, [name withheld]* has double glazing. He's less readable than a court order. But at least
you can ignore a court order. This guy's everywhere. This is a
man who does most of his acting with his teeth. Goddam that
flat-stomached, smooth-assed bastard.

See: SOME OTHER GUYS FOR A CHANGE

* The actor in question is a frequently named party in Gordy's last deposition
– *Ayo*.

*'You gotta have faith . . .'*

# FAITH

When forgiveness becomes impossible, the greatest gift you can give someone is FAITH.

Faith in their talent.

Faith in their potential.

Faith in their testimony.

That no matter what their eyes told them was real, it could well have been a trick of the light.

Think of the people who've shown faith in you.

Didn't take long, did it?

We remember those who showed faith in us. We remember them for the rest of our lives. People who look deep inside, peer past the poor credit history and see the man your father wouldn't let you be. And we remember the thousands who have scorned us just as vividly, be they studio execs, faculty heads or the morally conservative parents of girls who weren't even minors in some parts of Europe.

That's why acts of faith are so crucial in movies. In George Lucas's 1977 robots-on-the-lam dramedy *Star Wars: A New Hope*, Luke Skywalker (Mark Hamill) has to place his trust in The Force, even though it's a concept made up by George Lucas with no spiritual underpinning. When he shoots the laser into the hole bit that means the big black sphere thing blows up, everyone in orange is delighted. And so are we, not just because we know the film is nearly over now, but because the heart has won out over computer-guidance systems. Lucas, that great imaginer, managed to predict the frustrations of satellite navigation and how empty it feels when you arrive at your destination without having done anything yourself.

I've always driven without a satnav. Oftentimes I get lost, but when I get there (eventually) I know I've done it myself. I once had an argument with a woman over losing our way that was so bad she tried to suffocate me with the recently deployed air bag. But we *connected*. Now that woman is part of my legal team.

That's the power of cinema. That's the power of faith.

Goddam it if that other George* wasn't right.

You *gotta* have faith.

And it *would* be nice if I could touch your body.

* So now there are only two Georges? – *Ayo*.

# FAMILY

In movies, FAMILY comes first, yet few people in Hollywood can hold down a relationship because they're too busy making films about how important family is. Do you think *Mary Poppins* filmed itself?

# FEMALE DOCTORS/SCIENTISTS

In a movie's second half the FEMALE DOCTOR/ SCIENTIST may take off those large glasses to reveal her beauty. At this point the HERO may give her the gift of his private length.

But the glasses *must come off*. Glasses are an impenetrable barrier to the audience's affection. Name one movie star who wears glasses and isn't publicly regarded as a degenerate.

In Rowdy Herrington's 1989 doorman dramedy *Road House*, we first see Doc (Kelly Lynch) in 'professional' mode. She is treating top-class bouncer James Dalton (Patrick Swayze) for stab wounds incurred while shaking down a piece of shit in a bar. Her hair is in a plait and she is wearing large glasses – a total boner killer. But, as someone pertinently remarks later, 'That girl's got entirely too many brains to have an ass like that.'

Next time we see Doc, she's wisely let down her hair and lost the lenses.

It won't be long before she receives Dalton's secret meat.

See: DEVIANCY, GLASSES AS INCONTROVERTIBLE SIGNIFIER OF; HERO, THE

# FEMINISM

In Richard Fleischer's 1985 medieval dramedy *Red Sonja*, the titular heroine and would-be warrioress (Brigitte Nielsen) tells Lord Kalidor (Arnold Schwarzenegger) that she 'doesn't need a man's help'. Some critics see this as a FEMINIST statement.

But when she's surrounded by a large group of warriors seeking to avenge their slain master, who comes to her aid?

When a mechanical sea serpent sends her cowering into a crevice, who leaps in and wrestles the confounded beast?

When a portcullis doth threaten to crush her, who halts its descent with an arm that out-circumferences her womanish waist?

When an uncredited guard hastens to fasten his dev'lish trident betwixt her girlish shoulder blades, who smites that guard with the powerful thrust of his broadsword?

When her lust o'er-spills near the film's last breath, who is there to sate it?

And who gets top billing *above* the titular heroine?

Your boy Kalidor.

# FEMMES FATALES

FEMMES FATALES speak in low, sarcastic voices and rarely offer constructive feedback. They smirk, smoke and slink about the joint, barely displaying gratitude when the HERO gives them the gift of his secret length. As a result, we are seldom sad when they die in Act III.

See: HERO, THE; WELCOME DEATH OF THE SARCASTIC, THE

# FILM THEORY

A 'film' is made by a 'director'. For the purposes of reality, let's assume this director is a man.

Before each film, the director decides what he wants to 'say'.

He then communicates this 'vision' by pointing at other people and telling them what to do.*

Then he takes all the credit.

No one really likes films. Except for directors.

A 'movie' is made by a 'studio'.

Studios hire actors they think the public still likes to act in a story that's like something the public used to like three years ago. Then they hire a director who once made a good film to take the blame if it all goes wrong. If it's successful, everyone takes credit, except if it's a female director, in which case she probably just got lucky or blew someone. But if it all goes wrong and the director is female, it's totally her fault.

Everyone likes movies. Except for directors.

* Even though *he* cannot do anything that *they* do – *Ayo*.

# FIRST LINES

This ain't about transitioning from your chosen gateway drug to the good stuff. This is about dialogue.

In other words,* do you have a good opening?

Let's examine the beginning of Peter Hyams's 1994 sci-fi procedural *Timecop*. Its two themes are TIME and BEING A COP, so let's take a look at how this movie's first scene, without being heavy-handed, introduces them.

Walker (Jean-Claude Van Damme) approaches Melissa (Mia Sara) outside a shop. A clock is deftly foregrounded.

```
                    WALKER
         There's never enough time.


                    MELISSA
         Never enough for what?


                    WALKER
         To satisfy a woman.
```

Three lines. That's all it takes.

---

* I always think that if you're using the phrase 'in other words', why did you need the first set of words? – *Ayo*.

Thesis. Antithesis. Synthesis.

Thesis: we establish Walker as a philosopher, an inquirer looking at the whole Continuum of Finitude,* always craving more. But right away he meets his . . .

Anithesis: we establish Melissa, with her sassy retort, 'Never enough for what?', as a strong, independent woman who isn't afraid of speaking her mind. The fact that she's got a rocking bod is just so much gravy.

Synthesis: the radical, ultimately post-feminist notion that in a society where men are increasingly time-poor, we might be better off focusing on our own pleasure rather than wasting valuable man-hours on that ultimate oxymoron: the female orgasm.

See: BEING A COP; TIME

* Discarded James Bond title? – *Ayo.*

# FOREIGN FILMS

FOREIGN FILMS are any NON-AMERICAN MOVIE. To be born foreign is one of the great tragedies of life.

Sometimes you can get a really hot Brazilian chick, but she's never going to sound *right*. She'll always sound like something got stuck in her throat, and you can only perform the Heimlich maneuver so many times before you're asked to leave the restaurant. Because that's not a real doctor's bag.

Foreignness was less of a problem in the silent era. SILENT ASS knew no borders. Especially if that silent ass was WHITE. But as soon as we get into the business of chitty-chat, when we start talking *talkies*, sounding anything other than American becomes a hell of a problem, unless your tits go into next week.

British actors are often cast as villains. This is because there's something inherently evil about not being American. There's an uncanniness to seeing someone look like they could be a relatable white American, and then their mouth opens and this tight-ass *noise* comes out.

There is a small exception w/r/t some Celts – e.g. me/Sean Connery, in which cases virility trumps ethnicity.

See: BORDERLESS ASS; WHITE SILENT ASS
Don't see: NON-AMERICAN MOVIES

# FUCK

FUCK may be the most important word in cinema.

Which is more urgent?

'Let's get out of here!'

or

'Let's get the fuck out of here!'

Too fucking right.

Some sentences don't even make sense without the word 'fuck'. Take the line 'We're totally fucked'. Without the 'fucked' the sentence is a nonsense and has zero plot function. Sometimes the presence of the word 'fuck' is implied, as in 'What the – ?' This person was not about to say, 'Dickens'! In fact, if a word is deliberately missing in a screenplay, you can *assume* that the word is 'fuck'.

So can simply adding the word 'fuck' and/or derivatives of the word 'fuck' help your screenplay?

Fuck, yes.

Take the standard movie phrase 'What the fuck?' If someone is REALLY angry, try 'What the fuckin' fuck?'

But be cautious. The rule of 'three' does not apply. 'What the fuckity fuckin' fuck?' is one fuck too much and could risk making your character seem indecisive.

The prominent film critic Pauline Kael once claimed, 'The words "Kiss Kiss Bang Bang", which I saw on an Italian movie poster, are perhaps the briefest statement imaginable of the basic appeal of movies.'* But those were simpler, less good times.

Now, any decent action film could be summarized as: FUCK ME? FUCK YOU!

See: FUCKS, IMPLIED

---

* Surely 'Kiss Bang' would be more succinct? – *Ayo*.

# G

*'Try doing any of these things while keeping your ass still . . .'*

# GENRE

Filmmakers are sometimes called storytellers. But they're really salesmen, a dwindling special-interest group with a rapidly dating set of non-transferable skills looking to self-sustain. What are they selling? Stories. But who the hell wants to buy stories? Stories are long and boring. How do you get any right-thinking American to sit in a dark room and listen to a bunch of made-up shit?

You have to promise it's going to contain something interesting – like violence or tits.

Paul Verhoeven's 1990 time-travel dramedy *Total Recall* is such a great GENRE film that in one particularly memorable scene you get a bonus tit. That's why when Verhoeven came back with his 1992 ice-pick-com *Basic Instinct*, we knew we could *trust* him to deliver.

Am I gonna get violence?

Yes.

Am I going to get tits?

Yes.

What else you gonna give me?

Wait till the interrogation scene.

When do you think you'll start printing money?

Opening weekend.

What do you get when you watch a Mike Leigh film? Nothing. Except the uncomfortable feeling that a group of actors have been denied a writing credit.

This is why genre is so useful. It tells you *exactly* what service you are going to receive. Imagine going to a restaurant that didn't have pictures of the various dishes they serve. How would you know what you wanted to eat!? It's the same with movies.

And by the way, the one type of food no one in the world would ask for is British.

The same goes for the movies.

See: VIOLENCE + TITS = BUSINESS
Don't see: BRITISH FILMS

H

'*In movies, we seek the freedom
we lack in life . . .*'

# HERO, THE

The HERO rarely has need to apologize.* Women may demand an apology *from* him, but this is because they have misunderstood something, lack a key piece of information or, frankly, are just being MOODY WOMEN. More often than not, it is *they* who will later apologize for *their* misjudgment, at which point the hero will forgive *their* WOMANLY WEAKNESS. This frequently leads to LOVEMAKING. Lovemaking that is better than she could have ever imagined. Not that she's been with a butt-load of dudes or anything (because the hero must never end up with a SLUT); she's just a woman who INTUITIVELY APPRECIATES HIGH-QUALITY BEEF.

A hero should care about his hair, but not too much. It's rare to see a hero use a blow-dryer on screen, despite the fact that there's no way Kurt Russell isn't blow-drying his hair. I mean, how else does he get that kind of volume?

A hero cannot have curly hair. The hero's coiffure of choice is the mullet, which in many ways enshrines the Duality of Man: business up top, party down below. The mullet is the centaur of hairstyles: a mythical follicle waterfall.

Heroes are distinguished by their easy-to-understand payment plans. In Rowdy Herrington's 1989 exploration of doorman subculture, *Road House*, Dalton (Patrick Swayze) is a 'cooler' – an

---

* Gordy once made me apologise for forcing him to punch me – *Ayo.*

expert doorman known for his preternatural ability to manage bar-based conflict. His fee? '5,000 up front, 500 a night, [plus] all medical expenses.' A bargain! Especially given that he'll stitch up minor stab wounds himself.

The hero always asks for 'expenses', but he rarely keeps till receipts.

The hero will not enjoy a glass of wine with food. Wine is for villains in polo necks, sitting behind large desks, picking at exotic fruit and making undermining comments to subordinates.

The hero can drink large volumes of alcohol, yet remains safe to drive, something which the law blindly refuses to recognize. Those who refuse a dram cannot be trusted: they're calculating psychopaths unwilling to get into good-natured bar fights, spit at accented authority figures or safely swerve a car through night's dark embrace.

The hero's time is always running out, so when he drinks alcohol, he's going to make sure that it's as concentrated as possible. That's why the hero drinks spirits. In Ernie Barbarash's 2012 kidnapping dramedy *Six Bullets*, Samson Gaul (Jean-Claude Van Damme) drinks vodka throughout the first act, trying to block out the fact that he once accidentally blew up a couple of minors. In Joseph Zito's 1984 Viet-com *Missing in Action*, Colonel James Braddock (Chuck Norris) wakes up in a hotel room after an extended flashback of his time in North Vietnam. He has a BEER FIRST THING and then, in the tradition of the hero's innate distrust of tableware, drinks SPIRITS STRAIGHT FROM THE BOTTLE. You think complete intoxication will interfere with his CONCERTED ASS-KICKING? Fuck no!

The hero frequently receives dressing-downs from uptight stuffed shirts hiding behind desks. These by-the-book guys will soon learn that you can't win a war by sitting on your ass. You do it on the field. And the only true rule book is written on your heart.*

Heroes, once they've safely breached the compound, typically remove their fake mustaches/beards and discard them then and there, despite the fact that those fake mustaches/beards could have been soaked in alcohol and reused. Which is a shame/ pretty wasteful actually.

Heroes are always good with their hands. This is why they often prefer to stitch up their own wounds. In Félix Enríquez Alcalá's 1997 eco-thriller *Fire Down Below*, Jack Taggart (Steven Seagal) is so good with his hands that he is able to go undercover as a carpenter. As well as blowing the cover of a shady corporation implicated in toxic-waste dumping, racketeering and murder, he also manages to complete a new roof, reboard a porch, fix some rickety steps and build new beehives from scratch to replace the ones previously burnt by his love interest's psychopathic brother. If the hero of your film can't build a porch from scratch, perhaps it's time to take another pass.

The hero does not judge prostitutes. In fact, he shows them kindness, refuses to judge and will do anything to help them out of their predicament. He rarely forms a romantic relationship with one, though, because – well, once a whore always a whore.

The hero has seen more death than most. As he watches life slip from a minor character's body, he gives a slight bow of the

* Impairing legibility? – *Ayo.*

head, followed by a wince that could just as easily be explained by abdominal discomfort.

The hero is an excellent driver. This becomes particularly apparent when someone tries to ram his car off the road. Presumably these situations can't be frequent, so there would be virtually no opportunity to practice, but the hero instinctively knows exactly how to do it, even when using gearshift cars. It's difficult enough to maintain clutch control at traffic lights, especially if someone behind you is obviously impatient, let alone in near-death situations!

Heroes accept refreshments gracefully, particularly caffeinated hot drinks (a mug's fine). Alcoholic beverages (beer/grain-based spirits as opposed to wines/liqueurs) are acceptable at the end of a long day's work, but not during the middle of an assignment. The hero must refuse refreshments from a villain, lest the refreshments contain villainy. Similarly, he must never take a cigar proffered by a genocidal maniac, even if he really wants that cigar. The hero welcomes sustenance (a tin plate is fine) but won't accept treats such as ice-cream sandwiches, chocolate logs or gobstoppers. The hero must never be too full to beat someone to death.

The hero refuses to wear a tie, even in Europe.

The hero refuses to do up the top button of his shirt. But he'll never leave the whole shirt open – he's not a Mexican gang member.*

---

* Sometimes I wonder whether life would be simpler if I joined a gang, but then I remember that I don't look good in bandannas. So I have to scrap it out on the streets, solo – *Ayo.*

Heroes hate wasting time. 'You're wasting my time,' they'll say. Yet they devote very little time to time management, and rarely consult a diary.

The hero often struggles with relationships, but no one loves their children more than him. His work makes demands that his wife could never understand, and this leads to separation, though the sexual attraction she feels for him will never wane.

The hero is drawn to HOMELY HOTNESS. OVER-WHELMINGLY HOT WOMEN can't be trusted, even though they're really hot.

The hero is great with kids. Especially sick kids. And not only do all kids like the hero, they *respect* him. They sense his honesty. Even if he had to lie to them. Because a lie from a hero is part of a bigger truth that only he can understand. It is often hard for the hero to spend time with his own kids, though when he does, there's so much more in those two or three minutes than all the other stiffs and stuffed shirts manage with their decades of so-called 'consistent parenting'.

A hero should not own anything that he cannot carry with him while diving out of an exploding 'copter: e.g. lockets containing pictures/hair of dead wives; photos of estranged children; portable/autographed sporting memorabilia; small items that facilitate killing.

Heroes are loyal, but would never use a loyalty card.

See: ASS-KICKING, CONCERTED; DAUGHTERS; HIGH-QUALITY BEEF, WOMAN'S INTUITIVE APPRECIATION OF; HOTNESS, HOMELY; HOTNESS, OVERWHELMING;

INIQUITY, REFRESHMENTS FILLED WITH; LOVEMAKING;
MEXICAN GANG MEMBERS; PACKING SMART FOR A
REVENGE MISSION; SELF-RESTRAINT, HEROIC; SLUTS;
SPIRITS STRAIGHT FROM THE BOTTLE, IMPRESSIVENESS
OF THE HERO'S ABILITY TO DRINK; WOMANLY
WEAKNESS; WOMEN, MOODY

# HOTNESS

Hotness ain't about core temperature. Actors with excess body heat are not 'hot'. A movie actor can be feverish, his back tacky with brine, but the audience may remain unmoved.

Hotness is an index of *allure*.

So why do actors have to be so alluring? In what way does an actor's attractiveness improve the story?

By helping us give a damn.

It's very hard to care about ugly people. Looking at an ugly person is a BUMMER. Looking at an attractive person is great! Sometimes you can get an erection just by looking at an attractive person! What a gift an erection is! You can't get an erection from looking at an ugly person! In fact, your current erection might disappear! Who knows when you'll be able to get another one? It could be years! Before you know it, you're crying and you start to think, 'I can't stop! I'm going to be crying *for ever*!'

All these emotions distract us from the story. But when you see someone who's attractive, you can't take your eyes off them. Sometimes you'll start following them – spying on them, even! And what is a movie other than a bunch of people agreeing to let another bunch of people spy on them for a fee?

That said, there *are* movies that don't star attractive people.

We even have a name for them.

FLOPS.

See: BUMMERS; FLOPS; HOMELY HOTNESS

# HOUSING

In Rowdy Herrington's 1989 doorman dramedy *Road House*, Dalton (Patrick Swayze) is an expert bouncer or 'cooler', one of the best on earth. Yet he lives in a place with no TV, phone or air conditioning. The joint is so hot he has to make love on the roof.

In movies, we seek the freedom we lack in life, which is why we will never root for a HERO who signs a long-term rental agreement.

See: HERO, THE; LONG-TERM RENTAL AGREEMENTS, UNHEROIC NATURE OF; MAKING LOVE AL FRESCO ON AN INCLINE

# I

*'Some movies require interpretation . . .'*

# ILLITERACY

It is often said that film is a medium for ILLITERATES. I guess the idea is that shit-kickers like us find it easier to look at pictures than read books.

So does that make restaurateurs illiterates? *Their* menus have pictures in them. Or would it be more 'sophisticated' if they just *described* the different kinds of tacos?

How's about radio? Folks listening to the wireless are so dumb they call in with their opinions! How can I judge what you're saying when I can't see your face? For all I know you've got little piggy eyes!

Or ice hockey – you think those assholes are smart? They could do the exact same thing on grass, a surface that isn't *lethal*. These tubs of fuck are doing something so straight-ahead stupid that they have to wear full body armor. You wear less protection fighting a *fire*. An act which is, at least, necessary.

If a picture is worth a thousand words, and movies run at twenty-four frames a second, then the average Steven Seagal film works out at nearly 173 million words, or 1,728 books by Robert Ludlum.

So who you callin' illiterate now, motherfucker?

See: MOTHERFUCKERS, ILLITERATE-CALLIN'

# ILLNESS

HEROES rarely get ill, though they are frequently poisoned by cowards.

In McG's terminal ILLNESS dramedy *3 Days to Kill*, CIA agent Ethan Renner (Kevin Costner) develops a hacking cough during a routine sting operation. But what looks like a character 'quirk' or, worse, an attempt to imbue the movie with 'realism' thankfully turns out to be an advanced brain tumor.

Renner decides to quit the agency and use his remaining time on earth to reconnect with his daughter, Zooey (Hailee Steinfeld), and (less urgently) his ex-wife, Christine (Connie Nielsen), neither of whom knew about his covert life as a badass making the world a safer place one kill at a time.

But when elite CIA assassin Vivi Delay (Amber Heard) offers Renner an experimental drug that could prolong his life, he agrees to sign up for one last hit. A side effect of the serum is strong hallucinations, which, as well as giving director's director McG further license to bring his visual A-game, confirms that it's far better for a character to be drugged than ill.

Illness is a sign of weakness, which is gross and un-American – there's not much you can do about a cold apart from take a month off work and get tight in your car. Intoxication gives you something to fight against. Even if that fight is just with your bladder.

Further, it's better that the hero be *dying* than *ill*. There's dignity in bleeding to death by the harbor. Where's the dignity in chronic wind?

See: HERO, THE; WIND, CHRONIC

# INDEPENDENT FILM

Those who work in INDEPENDENT FILM are different to those who work in MOVIES. People who work in movies make movies for THE AUDIENCE.

People who work in independent films make films for People Who Like Independent Films. But People Who Like Independent Films are too busy to watch Independent Films because they're all making Independent Films of their own.

Perhaps this is an exaggeration.

There *is* a small audience for independent film. They sit during the early show in tiny, near-empty theaters, drinking white wine from plastic cups, silently consuming artisanal popcorn, letting it dissolve slowly in their liberal-leaning mouths and chewing only at moments when the film's soundtrack might mask their mastication, which is only once or twice because the film couldn't afford a proper score.

But if they were really honest with themselves, wouldn't they rather be at home rewatching *Bad Boys*?

No movie can be truly independent. It's *dependent* on people wanting to watch it.

See: AUDIENCE, THE; MOVIES

# INTERPRETATION

'All hands on deck' does not mean 'everyone touch the floor'. The phrase requires INTERPRETATION. It's one of the reasons I never cut it in the navy.

Sometimes MOVIES require interpretation.

No one wants to watch those movies.

On one level, Steven Spielberg's 1975 creature feature *Jaws* is about a shark trying to eat people. The fact that it has no other level is why it's so popular.

If your movie has 'subtext', you've got two choices: get rid of it or shift that shit up to the surface.

See: COMMANDS, AMBIGUOUS; MOVIES

# J

*'If only life were just . . .'*

# JESUS

Does not work as a screen character.

We cannot relate to him. He has no flaws.* What does he learn? Where's the love interest? Whither the arc?

That's why the best Christ biopic is told from Judas's point of view. Now here's a guy with a dilemma.

Timmy Rice knew this.

That's why he's a rich man.

Unlike JESUS.

There's a similar problem with J.C.'s Old Man. The Big Guy. The Silent Mover. And I ain't talking about air biscuits. Cos when He intervenes, it's *deus ex machina*.

*Deus ex machina* ain't the name of a metal band;** it means that some things happen not because the HERO willed it, but because they are beyond human control. And that just don't feel right.

No one's gonna pay double-figure dollars to see a film where the hero doesn't get exactly what he wants.

See: HERO, THE; *JESUS CHRIST SUPERSTAR*

---

* Maybe he cares *too* much? – *Ayo*.
** It's actually the name of an Italian progressive-rock band – *Ayo*.

# JUSTICE

One of the things that bind us to Steven Seagal is his sense of JUSTICE and how quickly he's able to enforce/apply it. Not for Seagal the bureaucratic machinations of an antiquated legal system and it's interminably slow 'due process', wherein people are 'innocent until proven guilty'.

Steven Seagal knows you're guilty. And he's going to apply on-the-spot physical sanctions.

This is kung fu justice.*

If you question why Steven Seagal is taking your car, innocent bystander that you supposedly are, he will kick you in the face. And he'll be completely justified in doing so!

This is hot-in-pursuit justice.

And when things have calmed down a little, Steven Seagal will reward the attractive woman's pliancy with the gift of his private length.

This is romantic justice.

If only life were just.

See: LIFE, STUPID

---

* Before you get the green ink out, Gordy won't acknowledge 'aikido', which he says sounds like 'painful bread' – *Ayo*.

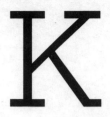

K

*'All these men have killed and killed again . . .'*

# KILLING

Can you think of a major motion-picture star who hasn't KILLED someone in a film?

Cruise
Seagal
Eastwood
Stallone
Statham
Cage
Bronson
De Niro
Pacino

All these men have killed and killed again. The only consistent non-killer among major movie stars is Woody Allen, which is one of the reasons why no one's ever really trusted him.

See: NON-VIOLENT MEN, INHERENT CREEPINESS OF

# L

*'Words have meanings . . .'*

# LANGUAGE

Words have meanings. They evoke images.

Take a Tuna Melt. It always conjures up some sub-Dalí tableau of fish wilting on a bent clock next to a dude with blood coming out of his tits.

So I can't eat them!

Even though, more often than not, they're the only thing my young girlfriends say they can make. But why would I want a 'mean' *anything*?

Film LANGUAGE *is* images.

A shot of a movie star leaves no room for interpretation. Here is a handsome man doing his best to remember, in often very confusing circumstances, which quip he needs to make after this other, less-well-paid person's done with the exposition.

# LOGLINE

Sounds like a subway system made of turd, but a LOGLINE is actually a condensed description of a movie, i.e. what is this story when you strip it right back to the balls?

*Citizen Kane*: A Rich Kid with a booming voice (Orson Welles) goes into the newspaper business, walks away from some toxic relationships, makes a butt-load of money, and for some reason is never happy.

*The Godfather*: A Tiny Italian (Al Pacino) bunks off military duty, marries two hot women, inherits the family business, and for some reason is never happy.

*Star Wars*: A Bored Farm Boy (Mark Hamill) leaves his home with a couple of gay robots, learns how to make blue light shoot out of a metal tube, gets off with his sister and blows up an enormous spaceship because a voice in his head told him to. He's beyond happy.

Which one do you think Disney bought?

# M

*'In the meantime, let's sell some tickets . . .'*

# McGUFFIN

Sounds like a breakfast roll, but it ain't.

It's something that keeps people watching the movie, but is ultimately meaningless.

A movie star is a McGUFFIN.

# MEDIEVAL DRAMA

It is not possible to write a MEDIEVAL DRAMA screenplay without using the prefix 'be-'. Unless your characters, at some point, use the words . . .

bewildered
befriended
bedraggled
besmirched
beguiled
beheaded
bejeweled
beloved
bequeathed
beseeched
besieged
besmudged
bedeviled
bewhiskered
betrothed
or betrousered

. . . you may as well set the thing in space.

See: THE MEDIEVAL DRAMA SCRIPT: BEGETTING IT RIGHT

# MENTORS

In movies, MENTORS have an extremely important role, even though they rarely get top billing.

Actors love playing mentors because they get to portray characters who are not only always right, but also get to sit down a lot.[*]

Mentor exposition tends to take place in the same location, allowing the actor to finish all his scene-work in a day or two.

Mentors have few costume changes and it's easy to make the argument that the character would probably be staring off into the middle distance, right where a prop boy can be holding up lines on giant cue cards.

This is of particular use during the LONG ROUSING[**] SPEECH that many mentors get to deliver before we go into an ACT III ASS-KICK, and it can help the actor come to terms with the fact that he's now too old to be considered a leading man, i.e. 65+ (the cut-off for women is mid-twenties).

See: ACT III ASS-KICKS; LONG ROUSING SPEECHES, THE PYRRHIC CONSOLATIONS OF

---

[*] And if they do stand, often get to rest on a stick – *Ayo*.
[**] And plot-recapping – *Ayo*.

# META

What is META?

In Frank Coraci's 2006 fantasy saga *Click*, Michael Newman (Adam Sandler) is an overworked architect who gets a 'universal remote control' that allows him to fast-forward to his career goals, while bypassing the tedium in between. But in so doing, he finds that he has missed many valuable life lessons.

On the surface, *Click* is a more satisfying iteration of Frank Capra's vastly overrated Jimmy Stewart actioner *It's a Wonderful Life* (*Click*'s 'universal remote control' resonates with a clarity far greater than the frankly trite 'angel' motif in *Life**), but *above the surface*, in meta city, shit gets deep.

All of us who drunk-bought *Click* at a gas station had the same thought when we finally plucked up the courage to watch it: 'What's stopping *me* from just fast-forwarding to the end of this thing? Isn't that the exact kind of meta gesture that the savvy makers of this unique societal critique would applaud? But surely they haven't made a movie that we're meant to skip through? They have product-placement deals to honor. There must be another explanation. Perhaps by making the film so hard to watch they're making *us* see the world through Michael Newman's eyes. Life is incomprehensible, dull and brutal! Just like watching *Click*!'

* Agreed. A piss-poor *Scrooged* rip-off – *Ayo*.

See?

If we had fast-forwarded through *Click* – and by Zeus it was tempting – we would never have learned the true lesson that comes from watching *Click*.

There *is* no real reason to watch *Click*.

*That's* more meta than your momma.

See: MOMMAS, VARYING META LEVELS OF

## MORE THAN ONE ASIAN PERSON

In movies, it's fine to feature a group of ASIAN PEOPLE in a crowd – e.g. a reaction shot of 'coders' at a computer company – but it's unwise to have more than ONE as a featured/named character. This ain't cast in stone; this is cast-ing. By all means let's reassess in fifty years.

But in the meantime, let's sell some tickets.

See: DON'T HATE THE PLAYER, HATE THE PLAY

# MOVEMENT

Movies are MOVEMENT!

What's that grenade doing? It's *moving* into that cluster of FOREIGN NATIONALS.

What's that hand doing? It's *moving* the HOT GIRL's bra off.

What's that other hand doing? It's *moving* that MINOR VILLAIN's defenseless head into a wall.

They're *called* MOVE-IES, not TALK-IES!

See: FOREIGN NATIONALS; HOT GIRLS; MINOR VILLAINS

# MULTIPLE NARRATIVE

MULTIPLE NARRATIVE movies feature many story strands, often interwoven. This can be done well (*What to Expect When You're Expecting*) or with a sledgehammer (*Short Cuts*).

Such films require a unifying event at the end to tie all the characters together. In Kirk Jones's elegant 2012 pregnancy saga *What to Expect When You're Expecting*, it's childbirth – the literal answer to the title's implied question. This is great screenwriting, 'delivering' a denouement that makes good on the implied contract of a poster typeset in pink.

Contrast this with Robert Altman's bloated 1993 pest-spray dramedy *Short Cuts*. The film ends with an earthquake, but cutting to everyone shaking while you jiggle the camera does not amount to an effective emotional catharsis. He could at least have had one of the characters attend a bikini contest. What happened to all the bugs? Did we win? Plus, a film called *Short Cuts* should be less long.

See: PAUL THOMAS ANDERSON'S *MAGNOLIA* AND WHY A RAIN OF FROGS CAN'T REALLY BE CONSIDERED 'RAIN'

# MUSTACHES

The word 'mystery' comes from the Greek and means 'shut your mouth'.

Good advice for a leading man.

I'm paying you to pretend to kill large numbers of nondescript people who are racially different to me. If I want exhausting jibber-jabber, I'll remarry one of my ex-wives.

The word 'mustache' is from the same Greek root. That's because if a guy has a good enough MUSTACHE, he doesn't need to talk. Look at Tommy Selleck. The most expressive thing about him is his chest hair. Same with Burty Reynolds. Here's what Burt's mustache is telling you: making love with me is so powerfully transcendent you won't care about the horseshoe of spikey scrub between my nose and upper lip.

Eyes are the windows to the soul, but when you open your mouth, all we see are your rancid teeth, a decaying, chalk-yellow fence straining to contain a puffy, pink, algae-speckled bladder.*

Why d'ya think Jimmy Cagney spoke outta the *side* of his mouth?

See: NAZIS: WHEN FACIAL HAIR FAILS TO HUMANIZE

* I think he means 'tongue' – *Ayo*.

# MUSTY

Think of your favorite movie star.

Seagal.
Stallone.
Statham.

What do you think they smell like? Lemon mist?

Nah.

These guys are only hitting the tub if circumstances compel them.

I stood behind Seagal at a rodeo once, and believe me, that smell wasn't coming from the bulls. He turned round and gave me a look like, '*You* deal with it.'

See: DEALING WITH IT RODEO-STYLE

# MYSTERY

How come wet wipes won't break down? How come something that you use on *babies* won't dissolve in *acid*, when your fucking car, which is supposed to be made of metal, dissolves in *drizzle*?

Why do these entitled college girls think they can mooch around all day on *my* futon, crunching up *my* pillow with *my* peanut butter, wipe their work-shy asses with *my* hard-won shit-tickets, and not contribute a dime?

How come I can't cry?

All these things are MYSTERIES.

Movies are built on 'em.

In an Ingmar Bergman film the mystery is: how did this icicle get funding? If I want to see the pale face of death challenge me to a board game, I'll take one of my ex-wives to a Cluedo convention.

In Orson Welles's 1941 snoozer *Citizen Kane* the mystery is: why did a rich kid name his sled after the clitoris?

In any David Fincher film the mystery is: who turned off all the lights? Did the meter run out?

In a Matthew McConaughey movie the mystery is: what do the top half of his eyes look like?*

* And when's he going to take off his shirt? – *Ayo.*

In a Nicolas Cage movie the mystery is: why are you trying to upstage *yourself*? There are no other professional actors in this film.

In a Steven Seagal movie the mystery is: how long will it take till everyone realizes he's entirely vindicated?

No mystery, no movie.

See: STEVEN SEAGAL, THE INEVITABLE AND COMPLETE VINDICATION OF

# N

*'In a movie, you just show the chair . . .'*

# NON-WHITES

It is very hard for audiences to connect with people who are NON-WHITE, unless they are Denzel Washington, who is so handsome that it doesn't matter. His handsomeness is like an event that *tricks you into forgetting he isn't white*.

In Joseph Zito's 1988 counter-communist dramedy *Red Scorpion*, we identify with the HERO, Nikolai Petrovitch Rachenko (Dolph Lundgren – a Swede), despite his sympathy-killing trait of being Russian, because most of the other characters in the film are either non-white or not played by Denzel Washington, thus *forcing* us to side with a Dirty Red. The remaining white people are either TOO FAT TO CARE ABOUT or even *more* Russian than our hero (heavily accented and sometimes weird-looking/bald).

In any case, Dolph Lundgren (one of the whitest action stars of all time – like the collective wet dream of a male-only Third Reich slumber party*) is functionally American: a tooled-up, monosyllabic Superman.

In movies, *nationality* is a state of mind: there are no borders/boundaries, as long as you ascribe to the values of the United States.

But race cuts to a narrative's heart. And narrative requires contrast.

* That snow-white hair, that oceanic stare! – *Ayo*.

If the good guy's black, what color's the villain?

See: ETHNICITY VS RELATABILITY; HERO, THE; MORE THAN ONE ASIAN PERSON; PEOPLE WHO ARE TOO FAT TO CARE ABOUT

## NOVELS VS MOVIES

The problem with NOVELS is that they're always describing things. But what is there to say about a chair?* It's hard to tell what one really looks like. All I know is the *feeling* of having my ASS halfway to the ground but for some reason not falling.

In a MOVIE, you just show the chair.

That's why I love 'em.

See: ASS; SHOW, DON'T TELL

* Or anything else? – *Ayo.*

*'Movies show us that our personalities
are essentially insignificant . . .'*

# OPENINGS

In John Irvin's 1986 crime-syndicate saga *Raw Deal*, we start with a sequence of pure cinema: powerful-looking men walking toward camera; speedboats skimming over sea; choppers cresting over hills; rifles with silencers; bags of drugs; men in suits stepping menacingly out of cars.

Compare this to the OPENING of Orson Welles's laughably overrated 1941 newspaper dramedy *Citizen Kane* ...

Some ancient fuck drops a snow globe.

Guess which one recouped. *Kane* is one of the few black-and-white films that couldn't even be saved by colorization.

Everything in the film is black and white anyway! Snow, doddery bores with white hair, newspaper print . . . The thing's deathly.

If you don't have a strong opening, how am I gonna trust you to handle the climactic shoot-out?

See: GETTING SHIT RIGHT UP TOP

# OPPOSITES

If you wanna create drama, you're gonna need OPPOSITES.

If you wanna create life, you're gonna need harmony.

That's why births come at the start of a movie, in order to *disrupt* harmony and *create* drama (*Look Who's Talking*), or at the *end*, to *conclude* the drama and signal *resolution/harmony* (*Rosemary's Baby*).

In Bruno Barreto's 2003 cabin-crew saga *View from the Top*, Donna Jensen (Gwyneth Paltrow) is considerate, ambitious and highly attractive. Whereas Ted Stewart (Mark Ruffalo) is considerate, relatively ambitious and highly attractive. It's the *contrast* between these two characters that drives so much of the story.

In Tom Vaughan's 2008 one-night-stand saga *What Happens in Vegas*, Jack Fuller (Ashton Kutcher) is a slacker who can't commit. Joy McNally (Cameron Diaz) is an uptight financial hotshot who can't let her hair down. But, crucially, they're very attractive. If one or both of them were ugly, the movie would be an abomination.

Movies show us that our personalities are essentially insignificant (we can change any key character trait simply by having a moment of revelation toward the end of Act II). What really matters is whether you have good bone structure. Because that can't change. If your kisser looks like a bag of dicks, you'll never find love.

Those without charisma and a low BMI are condemned to roam the earth for ever as a SUPPORTING CHARACTER or, worse, COMIC RELIEF.

See: CHARACTER, SUPPORTING; RELIEF, COMIC

# OSCARS, THE

Every year a group of super-old white people detain a group of super-attractive white people for four televised hours by distracting them with golden statues of a bald, penis-less man whose arms have melted into his chest.

THE OSCARS is the most important day in the Hollywood calendar. A billion people watch it, and it tells you everything you need to know about this business: without stories, Hollywood is just a bunch of giant-toothed white people with their hands down each other's pants.

And while we're at it, why isn't there a category for best female director? We don't expect an actress to operate at the same level as an actor, so why should we expect any more from a directress?

That's why no woman has ever won an Academy Award.*

See: DIRECTRESSES

* And I quote: 'Facts are for the weak' – *Ayo*.

# P

*'Some shit just don't make sense . . .'*

# PAIN

Have you ever had a penile fracture? It hurts. It's caused by sudden trauma to an erect penis.

Trauma can result from aggressive masturbation or misaligned penetration. Sometimes you'll hear a cracking sound. You may see dark bruising because blood's escaping from a ruptured cylinder. You may hear laughing because your partner's so drunk she's in hysterics.

You DO need urgent medical attention.

You DON'T need someone shining a torch on it so she can take a picture on her cellphone.

I've never seen a movie show this kind of PAIN. Real-life pain. The kind of pain that's hard to explain at Outpatients.

The movies exist as a way of *distracting* us from pain. That's why BRITISH FILMS are so unpopular.

(Don't) See: BRITISH FILMS

# PARADOX

How can you listen to Meatloaf's *Bat Out of Hell* AND 'observe the speed limit'?

Yet why would you listen to anything else in the car? You can't listen to Meatloaf anywhere *other* than a car. And why *is* this just 'my problem'?

Why are the real voices of 'comic' impressionists so unremarkable? Why, when they could adopt the voice of anyone else in the world, do they speak in *that* voice? Why don't they speak like Clint Eastwood *all* the time?

Why would anyone try to attack Steven Seagal? He's invincible.

Why do I run away when I feel love?

Why would anyone make a film starring Madonna when you could hire an actress?

Some shit just don't make sense.

We call that shit a PARADOX.

In Frank Coraci's 2006 handset dramedy *Click*, Michael Newman (Adam Sandler) is an overworked architect who is given a 'universal remote control' by the mysterious Morty (Christopher Walken) at the department store Bed, Bath, and Beyond. This device allows him to fast-forward to his career goals without having to go through the stress and repetition of daily existence.

But later he finds that, in so doing, he has missed many valuable life lessons.

But why doesn't Morty tell Newman that he's the angel of death *before* he gives him the remote control? That might have informed Newman's decision as to whether to accept it.

Why is Christopher Walken speaking as if he's live-translating his lines at a NATO conference?

Why isn't the angel of death focusing on killing people rather than on making periodical appearances during which he doles out increasingly logically-questionable exposition?

Why did I sit through the entire film only to find out that everything following Newman getting the 'universal remote control' from Bed, Bath, and Beyond is a dream?

These, too, are paradoxes.

The movies are *built* on them.

# PARTIES

The HERO hates PARTIES and will only attend one out of duty. Being open to joy/exhibiting signs of happiness is inherently repellent to the hero.

For the hero, happiness only exists in brief flashbacks to Super 8/B&W/video footage of the time when he was married, before he lost his wife in that unpreventable accident for which he blames himself, even though it totally wasn't his fault.

So he walks through sites of revelry with suspicion, trying to retrieve his naive daughter from the clutches of some piece of pond life – let's call him Chad. Sure, Chad's swagger may initially impress, but the daughter will soon realize what Chad's really after and reject his oleaginous advances, thus buying her old man enough time to bust down the door and kick this Chad punk into next week.

Pin-dicks like Chad, high on reefer and horny as hell, represent the worst aspect of masculinity: callow, young, hubristic. How far removed from the stately smolder of a man in the prime of his life (55–70)! Such a man – a real man – can truly protect a woman (17–35) who could become an excellent, fun stepmother to his daughter – they could even hang out like friends – so when he's busy they can sort of cancel one another out and stop beefing about how he's away the whole time, as long as they don't start going to . . .

See: ENJOYMENT, WHAT IS; HERO, THE

# POINT OF VIEW

Let us for a moment imagine the stories we could tell if cinema were ever to look at our world from a male POINT OF VIEW.

For the last seventy or so years, the industry has been pretty much a chicks-only affair. Occasionally a man (McG, Len Wiseman) gets to tell stories his way – but more and more it's stories about linen and chunky beads and salads and tearing little bits off baguettes and driving responsibly and being emotionally open and laughing with friends and being vulnerable over stoneware bowls of artisanal ice cream and it's driving me crazy my God some days I can't get up. I simply *won't get up*. Unless I feel myself starting to sway. Then I'll look out the window to see if I'm being towed.

See: IS IT ACTUALLY COMPLICATED, OR ARE YOU JUST MAKING A MEAL OF IT?

# POLO NECKS

The POLO NECK is an immediate, irrefutable indication of villainy.

The one exception is Illya Kuryakin (David McCallum) from *The Man from U.N.C.L.E.*, but that was episodic television – a completely different mythos! In fact, I think this is one of the reasons why Guy Ritchie's typically excellent movie reboot wasn't the box-office smash it should have been: people don't like to see heroes in knitwear. Knitwear suggests cosiness, complacency and inactivity; if an action hero is doing his job, he should look sweaty just standing in a vest. Think of how wet Bruce Willis gets in John McTiernan's 1988 hostage dramedy *Die Hard*. And that movie takes place at Christmas! Shit, that man's sexy. He gets so fucking wet I can't stand it.

In Tobe Hooper's underappreciated 1985 sci-fi slap *Lifeforce*, Col. Colin Caine (Peter Firth) saves humanity by staking one of the last surviving space vampires. And yet we never truly accept him as a HERO. This is because he insists on wearing a polo neck teamed with a trench coat – the go-to outerwear for the Third Reich.

I know what you're saying: 'Christopher Lambert, mother-fucker. Christopher fuckin' Lambert.' But he would soften the edgy fascism of his trench coat with a soft linen shirt.

The only thing that can take the edge off a polo neck is Steve McQueen and a shoulder holster.

See: CURLY HAIR; GUY RITCHIE, THE COMPLETE WORKS OF; HERO, THE; STEVE McQUEEN LOOKING SEXY AS SHIT WITH A GUN HOLSTER AND POLO NECK

# POSTERS

On the POSTER for Bruno Barreto's 2003 cabin-crew drama *View from the Top*, the 'I' in the word 'VIEW' is typeset to look like it's the symbol for a women's toilet. Straight away we're engaged, thrillingly, by a series of questions:

— Is the 'I' inherently feminized in modern society? Is the male ego, or 'I', redundant?
— Is the 'I' literally a toilet? A private place where you close the door and pull down your pants? A place to 'jettison' unwanted personal 'cargo' (feces, urea, etc.)?
— Had they just not thought about how weird it looks?

Clearly, this is a movie which challenges reason itself.

Posters must provoke!

# POST-TRAUMA SHOWERS

POST-TRAUMA baths are not cinematic. If you've just killed someone in a violent rage, the last thing you'll want to do is hop in the tub.

In Paco Cabezas's 2014 gangland execution dramedy *Tokarev*, Paul Maguire (Nicolas Cage) kills a Foreign National by repeatedly smashing his head into the ground.

Now he's sweaty and uncomfortable.

Wisely, he heads straight for an enormous shower stall, large enough to accommodate his full width.

Cabezas, a director who trusts his audience with an almost touching zeal, allows this moment to breathe, much like the pores on Maguire's massive back.

We must *presume* that Maguire has put on the immersion heater or has a tankless hot-water system, because as the droplets fall, ricocheting off his rhomboids, the last thing he'll want is to be jolted out of his 'oh-the-humanity' reverie by an icy gush. Skipping out of the shower shrieking, 'Holy shit, you guys, this thing's fucking freezing,' might make him look shallow.

And Maguire is not shallow. He actually feels pretty damn conflicted about smashing that man's skull. He'll have scratches on his knuckles for days: a haunting reminder of the all-too-fleeting nature of life and the awesome power contained within him – a power that he can and will unleash on anyone else who refuses to give him adequate intel.

Because when you think about it, what compelled Maguire to do what he did was injustice. Paul Maguire can't *stand* injustice.

He would probably love to walk away from injustice like everyone else, perhaps even profit from it, but he can't. He was born with an unerring sense of what justice is, and is able to do what it takes to enforce it on an ad hoc basis. Sometimes this will involve the death of others.

How can he justify these deaths?

It's *instinctive*.

We just have to trust that Maguire will *only kill when necessary*. Was this particular killing necessary? It was borderline. Hence the long shower. He's cross with himself. Perhaps there was no need to kick the man in the stomach with such force/frequency, but everything else was on the level.

So yes, it was necessary. That fat fuck whose head came apart in his hands wouldn't give him the intel he'd asked for, so that fat fuck had to go down. If he hadn't been such a pussy-ass fat fuck, he might be in a coma now instead of the morgue. That's not Maguire's fault. It's someone else's, i.e. the fat fuck's.

And okay, maybe (on second glance) repeatedly shooting him after he'd smashed in his head was excessive, but by that point he was dead anyway. Isn't it better that Maguire unleashes his fury on a corpse rather than on someone who's still alive?

Cabezas grants us the time to read all these thoughts into the landscape of Nicolas Cage's back.

Maguire stares at his hands as if he can't believe he *has* hands – as if they should have just dropped off from the shame. A weaker character would do an UGLY SNOT-CRY, while sliding down the tiles into a fetal position near the drain.

But Paul Maguire stands tall until the last of the guilt is hosed off.

See: THE COMPLETE WORKS OF STEVEN SEAGAL; WEEPING, UGLY/SNOTTY; WATER-SOLUBLE REMORSE

# POWER

All memorable films are about POWER.

But few memorable films have been made about power suppliers, despite the increase in so-called 'origin' stories.

See: GAPS IN THE MARKET, FINDING/EXPLOITING

## POWERFUL MEN VS THEIR WEAK SONS

POWERFUL MEN frequently have WEAK SONS. In Félix Enríquez Alcalá's 1997 eco-thriller *Fire Down Below*, Orin Hanner Jr (Brad Hunt) and Orin Hanner Sr (Kris Kristofferson) are discussing how to deal with Jack Taggart (Steven Seagal), an undercover Environmental Protection Agent posing as a handyman.

'Should I take him out?' asks Hanner Jr.

Hanner Sr's reply?

'You couldn't take out a cheeseburger from a drive-thru window.'

What Orin Hanner Sr fails to realize is that taking out a cheeseburger from a drive-thru window is actually quite easy. Indeed, the drive-thru window's sole purpose is to make this already-not-terribly-taxing transaction less onerous. This is a system designed for people who have concluded that one of the things preventing them from eating more cheeseburgers in-house is the exhausting walk from the parking lot to the counter.

Orin Hanner Jr almost certainly *could* take out a cheeseburger from a drive-thru window. In fact, this task would be far better suited to his limited abilities. How can Orin Hanner Sr seriously expect Orin Hanner Jr to physically combat Steven Seagal? No one on earth can 'take out' Steven Seagal! Has anyone even landed a punch on Steven Seagal?

So we can only assume that Hanner Sr's comment is not true. It is, in fact, a comic exaggeration intended to wound.

But if Hanner Sr has such little faith in his son's ability, why has he given him such a high level of responsibility within his criminal organization? Hanner Jr is essentially acting as Hanner Sr's deputy for much of the narrative! If Hanner Sr wasn't so busy at the casino or having hot women straighten his tie during business calls, perhaps his son would feel more motivated!

Has Orin Hanner Sr stopped to consider the impact of selfishly privileging his own feelings of negativity and hostility? How's he meant to build up trust within his crime syndicate if his henchmen don't feel loved and nurtured? If that's how he speaks to his son, they might ask, imagine how sardonic he might be with *us*!

When people are unfairly maligned, their self-esteem plummets, they doubt the love of the person criticizing them and they become defensive. Sometimes they're so upset they feel compelled to get a tattoo of a Celtic symbol as a badge of their individuality. So if you say to someone, 'You can't even take out a cheeseburger from a drive-thru window,' perhaps that person will start to believe that he's unable to perform other simple tasks – like breathing. Next thing you know, he's writhing on the floor and choking for no reason! How's he meant to rough up rival criminals when he's thrashing on the deck like a beached haddock?!

And this is to say nothing of the damage Orin Hanner Sr is doing to himself as a parent. He's continually eroding the bond of trust between himself and his child. By making statements that aren't true, or not *meant*, he's actually de-authorizing himself as a leader and a father. He's showing that his judgments are wildly inaccurate! Nonsensical even! How is Orin Hanner Sr modeling leadership for Orin Hanner Jr, should Orin Hanner Jr get to run his own crime syndicate? He's not!

If this gang is to succeed in the criminal world, they're going to need incredible tenacity, because there's *so much* resistance to gangs from 'legitimate' elements in society. People often react negatively to hoodlums ('You're hurting me,' 'I'll make you pay for this,' 'I'm going to avenge my son,' etc.), so henchmen really have to believe that what they're doing is both necessary and *valuable*. If they feel like they can never please their boss (no matter how hard they try!), why should they put in any effort at all?

By undermining his son, the powerful father ends up making himself weak . . .

I am the strong one, Dad.

Me.


See: CRIME SYNDICATES, BUILDING SELF-ESTEEM WITHIN

# PRISON RAPE

In Félix Enríquez Alcalá's 1997 eco-thriller *Fire Down Below*, Jack Taggart (Steven Seagal), confident of the impending incarceration of antagonist Orin Hanner Sr (Kris Kristofferson), contends that he knows someone in PRISON called Tyrone who will probably RAPE him.*

In Rowdy Herrington's 1989 doorman dramedy *Road House*, the villainous Jimmy (Marshall R. Teague, appearing under the not-entirely-effective pseudonym Marshall Teague) tells Dalton (Patrick Swayze), 'I used to fuck guys like you in prison.'

How come the rape threat in *Fire Down Below* is such good-natured fun, while the rape threat in *Road House* is so heinous?

It boils down to consent.

Kris Kristofferson's Orin Hanner Sr is evil. Therefore, he wishes evil to prevail. Rape is evil. Therefore, Kristofferson's assent to rape can be assumed, even when he's the 'victim'. Seagal is literalizing the untenability of the villain's philosophical standpoint. Plus, while it's amusing to *threaten* rape, it's another thing to *actually do it*! And in any case, it wouldn't be Seagal doing the raping – it would be Tyrone! Taggart isn't personally implicated at all! He's just making a light-hearted

---

* Kristofferson's character, not Seagal! I'd like to see someone try to rape Steven Seagal! He wouldn't allow it! – *Ayo.*

observation of a likelihood (possibly) based on past experience/
hearsay!

In commercial cinema, the *way* you threaten rape is crucial.

See: RACIAL STEREOTYPES, NAMES INTENDED TO EVOKE;
RAPE, FUN WAYS TO THREATEN

# PURE CINEMA

4(+) powerful men in vests walk toward us, the sweat on their massive arms reflecting the blood-red fireball behind them.

A speedboat skims the ocean like an expensive stone. The driver pushes the throttle to the 'max', while his other lovely arm silhouettes his attack rifle against a blood-red sky.

Seven coal-black choppers crest over a blood-red sky, their pilots' bulging arms rippling invisibly in their sleek cockpits.

Three magical movie moments.

But what links them?

None of them have dialogue.*

In PURE CINEMA, there are no words. Only indelible images. Nothing more. Apart from action and sound effects and light.

And music helps.**

---

* Is that a link? Neither Heinrich Himmler nor Oprah Winfrey are Dutch nationals – *Ayo*.
** I concur. Images on their own can feel kind of ghostly – like say you're lying on the floor – the TV's on but it's muted – the speaker's been making a fizzing sound ever since you karate-kicked it – the remote's out of reach – you're too bruised to move – a cartoon comes on – and it feels creepy – these happy-looking animals being forced to speak English regardless of their species – but they can't convey loss – or anything like real pain – their recovery times are really rather fast considering these are quite serious injuries – they seem oblivious to death – the fact that we are dying every second of our lives – so you find yourself in the middle

See: HAILS OF EMPTY BULLET SHELLS; MASSIVE LOVELY ARMS; QUICKLY ASSEMBLING SNIPER RIFLES; SILENCERS AFFIXED TO THE TOP OF RIFLES; WOMEN IN CLINGY DRESSES STEPPING OUT OF SEXY CARS

---

of a soft howl and you let half an hour's worth of stored-up saliva fall from your mouth – *Ayo*.

*'Quitting is never acceptable . . .'*

# QUITTING

QUITTING is never acceptable in commercial cinema.

In John Irvin's 1986 crime-syndicate dramedy *Raw Deal*, FBI chief Harry Shannon (Darren McGavin) tells newly reinstated FBI agent Mark Kaminsky (Arnold Schwarzenegger) that he might quit. Shannon's legs were shot full of holes during a Mafia assassination attempt by the same people who murdered his son, Blair. Now he's so demotivated he refuses to even *try* to walk!

Kaminsky will not accept such moral cowardice: 'You don't have to walk, but you have to try like hell.' He then adds, cannily, 'Did you ever quit in front of Blair?' Presumably, FBI chief Harry Shannon never did, because without emitting so much as a slight grunt he manages to walk several steps before collapsing into Kaminsky's arms for a hug that is as non-sexual as it is life-affirming.

See: GOALS, USING MEMORIES OF A DECEASED RELATIVE TO HELP FOCUS ON ONE'S; 'HELL' AS MINIMUM REQUIRED EFFORT LEVEL

# R

*'You swallow the scorpion . . .'*

# REALITY

Movies are not REALITY.

In Orson Welles's 1941 clunker *Citizen Kane*, we discover that Charles Foster Kane (Orson Welles) could never be happy because he had a sled fetish. How do we know this? Because right before he dies, he says 'Rosebud' to his snow globe. Then it starts to snow in his *mouth*! Next thing we know, a bunch of young people dressed up as old people claim to be able to recall this sicko's life with photographic accuracy.

In John G. Avildsen's 1976 slugfest *Rocky*, a white person becomes a boxing champion!

In Roman Polanski's 1974 water-shortage saga *Chinatown*, there isn't a single scene in an Asian restaurant!

The whole thing is laughable!

But in Polanski's 1968 pregnancy dramedy *Rosemary's Baby*, Guy Woodhouse (John Cassavetes) allows the devil to inseminate his wife so he can get better acting roles.

Finally, something I can believe!

See: SNOW, HIGHLY IMPLAUSIBLE NATURE OF MOUTH

# RELUCTANCE

Think of how often a movie HERO displays RELUCTANCE.

He doesn't *want* to punch that man in the face; it's just that the son of a gun won't leave the hot woman alone.

He doesn't *want* to make love to the highly strung hot woman; it's just that it'll help her loosen up and stop being such a goddam tight-ass.

He doesn't *want* to be partnered with some slight, bookish-yet-hot woman who's just aced her last semester of cop school – she'll slow him down when shit gets real on the street; it's just that the smarts she'll learn from him in two minutes flat will help her more than a lifetime of theory. So what's he gonna do? Let her die in the 'hood like a miniature pig?

He doesn't *want* to endanger his life fighting for freedom – it's already cost him his marriage, his liver, and turned his chest hair ash-white; it's just that he's the best they've got.

The true hero doesn't want to do *anything* except finish up his bourbon. And yet when I act like that, people tell me I'm wasting my life. Or that's what their eyes are saying. Looking at me like a nothing. So I tell them, 'You don't know diddly shit about creating a protagonist through narrative structure. I do. I write new pamphlets every other year. I'm a hero. I'm a storyteller. I'm perfectly safe to drive.'

See: HERO, THE; MINIATURE PIGS, INCREASED RISK OF
DEATH W/R/T

# RESCUE

If someone RESCUES you, you cannot be a HERO. You are most likely a child or an above-averagely-attractive woman.

As such, Solomon Northup (Chiwetel Ejiofor), the titular protagonist of Steve McQueen's 2013 plantation dramedy *12 Years a Slave*, is not a hero.

The hero of that flick is Mr Parker, a shopkeeper who recognizes Solomon at the end of Act III and courageously suggests that someone else should free him.

But Parker is white, and in these politically correct times his heroism is downplayed by a media that would rather celebrate a central character who lacks the imagination to escape from a field. Clint Eastwood escaped from Alcatraz! Can you imagine a Bruce Willis movie in which he was captured, alternated between self-pity and stoic passivity, and *didn't* single-handedly execute everyone who stood in his way?

No wonder *Slave* didn't get a sequel.

See: HERO, THE; RESCUE, LEVELS OF ATTRACTIVENESS REQUIRED FOR

## ROCK BOTTOM

Every HERO hits ROCK BOTTOM.

It's 3 a.m., you're down to your last few burritos, you want to make some kind of connection with someone, but you're too blasted to get out of the tub. You feel something dripping on your head, revealing your bald spot. You look up: the shower head is on. How long have you been here? You look down and see a toe floating in the suds. When you realize it's still attached to your foot you start to cry.

You're on the freeway. For some reason you're moving. You can barely hold the wheel. You don't know why you're here. You don't know where 'here' is. Whose car is this? It smells of cement. Or maybe pork. Rain reveals your bald spot. You look up: why doesn't the car have a roof anymore? Didn't it used to have a roof when that other person was in the car? You look down and see that your pants are on the passenger seat. Now you're on a grass verge. It's possible that the car is upside down. Finally, you can rest your head on the dashboard. You look down, or is it up? Your exposed penis and thighs tumble toward your bleeding chin. Why do they look so bright? Why is everything flashing blue? What's that tapping on the window?

You're trying to sleep. You feel something funny in your arm. You see what looks like a lit cigarette singeing your hair, but when you pick it up to take a drag you realize it's a scorpion.

You swallow the scorpion, but it tastes like a lighter. The wind reveals your bald spot. You look up. That's not wind. That's paraffin. Someone's trying to set fire to your dumpster. How are you going to sleep if this thing catches? You've lost your faculty card and you don't have the energy to beg. So you close your eyes and hope the puke will staunch the flames. You look inside but all you can see is you and you and you and you, all jerking each other off in an octagon.

For the hero, things do not end here. Act III's round the corner.

It's time to scrape off the vom and KICK SOME ASS.

See: ASS-KICKING, CONCERTED; HERO, THE

# S

*'You just gotta keep checking for shards . . .'*

# SCIENCE FICTION

The tagline to Ridley Scott's 1979 sci-fi dramedy *Alien* is:

*In space, no one can hear you scream.*

Then how come we can hear the dialogue?

In George Lucas's 1977 farmers-in-space saga *Star Wars*, it's not the stars that are doing the fighting. It's the *people*.

And why can't I remember anything about the plot of *Total Recall*? The story is so unmemorable that Len Wiseman filmed the movie *again* in 2012 before anyone realized that Paul Verhoeven had already made it in 1990.

Upshot? SCIENCE FICTION and science fact are two very different animals. In fact, they're not even animals!

# SECRET AGENTS

In McG's 2014 brain-tumor dramedy *3 Days to Kill*, Ethan Renner (Kevin Costner) has kept his highly dangerous work in government ops a secret his whole life. His service to his country has cost him his marriage and estranged him from his daughter. So when elite CIA assassin Vivi Delay (Amber Heard) offers him an experimental drug that could prolong his life (on the condition that he terminates an arms trafficker called The Wolf), he faces a terrible dilemma. In order to ensure a future with his family, he must go back to his old life, but because he has to do it secretly, they'll never understand the sacrifice he's making! In fact, they give him hell about being late for stupid dinners or after-school pick-ups! When he almost got an ass full of lead!

Part of the film's success is that it recognizes how unappreciated men are in the modern world. This guy was literally out saving the planet, and all his ex can do is beef about how he wasn't around enough. Well, why don't *you* try telling a bunch of highly trained dissidents that you can't let the firefight go on *too* long because you've got to go home and listen to your wife complain about everyone she met that day?

The subtext of all SECRET AGENT movies is the impossibility of explaining anything to a woman. Because ALL men are secret agents. We're doing shit women will never understand: covert shit, dangerous shit, draining shit.

When there was a wasp crawling up your bikini strap, who told you to just stay still? Who de-iced the windshield before it was even noon? Who made two trips to the dump to get rid of a bunch of old shit you made me throw away even though we might one day need it? Who set up the new speaker system so that we can hear the bass properly? Who downloaded that app on your phone in under an hour? Who knew that there was an even cheaper restaurant only three miles' walk away?

Men knew, that's who.

The secret agent represents the part of male consciousness that women can never access – a world of speedboats, emptying full clips into Foreign Nationals and meaningless animalistic trysts with sultry hot tamales.[*]

Women don't understand that men *need* to do this in order to *make the world safe for them.* I'm not trying to slake the lust of every exotic woman in the world, but if I had to (for the sake of *international security*) give some knockout dame the gift of my private length, I would. I totally would. I'd *have* to.

Men like this, HEROES, are destined to walk through life alone, judged, scorned, misunderstood and saddled with alimony.

See: HERO, THE; SULTRY WOMEN, SELFLESS LUST-SLAKING OF

---

[*] It seems perverse that LaSure would not refer to James Cameron's seminal *True Lies*, a film based on this dichotomy. It's very possible that LaSure, a man who needed little excuse to rewatch *Road House*, had never heard of it – *Ayo*.

## SELF-LOVE

The tragedy of Narcissus is not that he fell in love with his own reflection; it's that he never learned to swim. Who hasn't tried to dry-hump a mirror? You just gotta keep checking for shards.

The true HERO knows he will never find his equal. If he did, he'd have to share billing.

Do you think Schwarzenegger, Stallone or Seagal would ever split their massive fees with some dame?

What for?

They've got their own tits.

See: HERO, THE; OWNING YOUR TITS (AS A MAN)

# SETTING

Where's your story *set*?

> A titty bar (*Showgirls*)?
> Various titty bars (*Striptease*)?
> An ancient titty bar (*Mrs Henderson Presents*)?

In which *era* is your story set?

> Post-apocalypse (*Mad Max*)?
> Mid-apocalypse (*Apocalypse Now*)?
> Pre-apocalypse (*He's Just Not That into You*\*)?

What are your characters fighting – what are they *set* against?

> Their ex-girlfriends (*Ghosts of Girlfriends Past*)?
> The outdated concept of monogamy (*Ghosts of Girlfriends Past*)?
> Matthew McConaughey's own self-worth (*Ghosts of Girlfriends Past*)?

Three crucial questions, three routes to world-beating movies (apart from *Apocalypse Now* – it's pretty sweet when they napalm the jungle, but after that it literally *drifts*).

See: JUNGLE, DIFFICULTY OF NARRATIVELY TOPPING NAPALMING A

---

\* I find this film's title has the unfortunate effect of making me imagine a mid-congress observation made by a third party. LaSure told me that he once received similar feedback from a gas fitter in Houston – *Ayo.*

# SEX

In Joseph Zito's 1984 action dramedy *Missing in Action*, Colonel James Braddock (Chuck Norris) goes back to his Saigon hotel room with the relatively hot Ann (Lenore Kasdorf), but when he removes his top to reveal his stacked and hairy torso – looking like a wet barrel that's been picked up from a barber-shop floor – it's not to make sweet love to her, although she waits in anxious anticipation of his length; it's to change into ninja blacks, scope out the city and ice a commie piece of shit.

HEROES never prioritize the carnal (except in Sharon Stone movies – she's like the Pied Piper of penis).

There'll be another sweet piece round the corner before your gun barrel's gone cold.

See: GUN-BARREL COOLING TIMES, APPROXIMATE;
HERO, THE; NINJA BLACKS; ROUND-THE-CORNER SWEET
PIECES; TORSO HAIR

# SHAKING HANDS

HEROES very rarely agree to SHAKE HANDS, and almost never air-kiss. And yet, despite their lack of civility, we cheer them on. This is because the hero acts as *we wish we could* and NOT *as we actually do. We* don't want to touch people's puffy hands; *we* don't want some asshole's clammy cheek barreling toward us in smug expectation; *we* don't want to endure the humiliation of having our outstretched arm pivoted back into our chest for a hip-hop hug from a forty-five-year-old. And yet we allow these violations every day of our shriveled lives.

Do you think Jason Statham would put up with this bullshit?

That's why we love him.

See: FAT-CAT TYPES, REFUSING CIGARS FROM; HERO, THE

# SHOWERS OF SPARKS

Have you ever seen a SHOWER OF SPARKS in real life?

That's why we go to the movies.*

* Or watch talent shows? – *Ayo*.

# SKIN

If you want to make a buck in this biz, someone's gotta show some SKIN.

But don't give 'em everything right up top; it's best to take her slow . . .

In Joseph Zito's 1988 action classic *Red Scorpion*, we have to wait thirty-eight long minutes until we see Dolph Lundgren's bangers; then it's an agonizing additional twenty-two minutes before we see his exposed legs in short cut-offs that detail his dense quads.

In John Irvin's 1986 lesson in action *Raw Deal*, we have to wait *seventy-two* minutes for a shot of Arnold Schwarzenegger's wet tits, still steaming from the shower.

In Rowdy Herrington's 1989 doorman thriller *Road House*, we have to wait way past the Act II mid-point before we see dappled spots of sun yellowing the sweat on Patrick Swayze's naked back, a shimmering pool of meat inviting us to dive ever deeper into his deltoids.

In *Barb Wire*, Pamela Anderson drops her melons in the title sequence. How are you gonna top that! Cut straight to an explosion? No wonder it bombed at the B.O.

Seeing Pammy act is the price you pay for the *prospect* of seeing her naked. As soon as we got that title sequence, there was no reason for us to see the rest of the film – you want to leave the theater, but you can't stand up.

The whole thing's a boner-killing mess.

# SLUT

A SLUT is a woman who has sex with someone other than the HERO.

An exception exists for a woman trapped in a loveless relationship wherein congress is perfunctory, off-screen and, as such, no real threat to the hero, with whom true, LIFE-GIVING, orgasmic BOOM-BOOM awaits.

See: BOOM-BOOM, LIFE-GIVING; HERO, THE; NON-HERO TYPES, CONSISTENT SEXUAL INADEQUACY OF; OBLIGATION, PERFUNCTORY CONGRESS WITH NON-HERO TYPE OUT OF A SENSE OF

# SNIVELING

Slapping a SNIVELING person is not, for some reason, assault.

## SON OF A BITCH

One of the few acceptable terms of endearment in cinema, it can also be used to indicate surprise ('Son of a bitch!') or a moment of realization ('*Son of a bitch . . .*').

Oddly, it is seldom used to denote a dog's lineage.

# SOUNDTRACK

Has there ever been a bigger missed opportunity than Terry Malick's 1973 serial-killer dramedy *Badlands*? Two kids in double denim shooting off guns just for yucks could have been backed by a kick-ass SOUNDTRACK. I'm thinking how Jovi took things Next Level on *Young Guns II: Blaze of Glory*.

Instead, we get the inane ramblings of some chick who sounds like she's about to go in for emergency oral surgery and is trying to distract herself from the pain by playing the waiting-room glockenspiel. And it's always the same tune! I love 'Livin' on a Prayer', but Jovi would never play it twice in a row! Part of the joy of hearing 'Livin' on a Prayer' live is that you know you won't have to hear it again until you're back in your truck.

Yet many so-called 'classic' films repeat the same theme again and again. (I'm looking at you, Georges Delerue: your 'score' to Jean-Luc Godard's *Le mépris* is *literally* a stuck record. Same deal with Carol Reed's 1949 antibiotic dramedy *The Third Man*. Not only can you barely see what's going on, it plays like an unfunny episode of *Curb Your Enthusiasm*.)

But soundtracks *can* be used to *subvert* expectations:

Try some space funk under that courtroom summation.
Underscore that sex scene with sounds from a squash match.

Use classical music under your diarrhea montage.

See: MUSICAL JUXTAPOSITIONS, TOTALLY RADICAL

# SPACE JARGON

When watching Tobe Hooper's 1985 space-vampire dramedy *Lifeforce*, I mistook the term 'soft dock' as a snide reference to impotence.

It is painful to be reminded of one's own failings. It's painful in court, it's painful when you're being held down by your current brother-in-law, it's especially painful at a press screening. And it can be crushing to be corrected by the director of that movie during a subsequent Q and A.

Point being, it doesn't take much to make me think of the few dozen times when I've been too filled with self-hate and rye to get the blood flowing to the right set of sacs.

So let's get it right. Here's a list of some useful SPACE JARGON from Joss Whedon's 2012 cash cow *The Avengers*:

> 'There's no one that knows gamma radiation like you do . . .'
> 'Your work on anti-electron collision is unparalleled . . .'
> 'We can clock this at 600 teraflops . . .'
> 'The portal is collapsing in on itself . . .'
> 'This is a level 7 . . .'

The writing is so strong that only the last few remind me of my intermittent leverage. You can also use the following stand-alone terms during nearly any hard SF* exchange:

---

* SF = science fiction. When an acronym necessitates a footnote, perhaps a rethink's in order? – *Ayo*.

calibrate
comms (off or on)
evac
initialize
intel
ion
partial evac (something I once had to do in an alley)
particle
probe
proton
thrust

Or combine them in virtually any order, e.g.:

calibrate comms
ion thrust
initialize partial evac module
etc.

Or try throwing 'anti-', 'auto-', 'hyper-' or 'nano-' into the mix,
e.g.:

auto-proton probe
anti-ion thrust
hyper-calibrate nano-comms
etc.

For reasons too painful to restate, avoid the prefix 'semi-'.

# SPEAKING VOLUMES

Regardless of the 'character' they're playing, Steven Seagal, Bruce Willis and Jason Statham rarely shout. In fact, they barely open their mouths. It sounds like they've had all the moisture syringed from their throats. Who knows if they even have tongues?

But actors of their stature, stubble and syllabic simplicity don't need to be audible. Why?

Because they have *power.*

Villains shout because, deep down, they're weak. Foreign Nationals speak loudly because, deep down, they're weak. Women scream at me because, deep down, they're weak.

Someone's voice level can SPEAK VOLUMES.

See: WOMANLY SHRILLNESS

# STAGING

In McG's 2014 modern classic *3 Days to Kill*, a dying CIA agent, Ethan Renner (Kevin Costner), is offered a life-prolonging experimental drug if he agrees to perform one last hit for the agency. During the course of his mission, he has to unravel the ass of an assailant at a cold-meat and cheese counter. And though the cheese remains unweaponized, Renner's face *is* pushed quite close to an electric meat slicer.

Imaginative staging like this creates a NEXT-LEVEL VIGNETTE that lingers in the memory long after you leave the theater. Where would YOU assault Kevin Costner?

A bubble-wrap factory?

A 'legitimate' massage parlor?

A blue whale's heart?

You're the storyteller. YOU choose.

See: ASSAULTING KEVIN COSTNER: WHEN, WHERE, HOW OFTEN; NLVs

## STANDING UP SLOWLY TO REVEAL SOMEONE'S TRUE HEIGHT

Despite the fact that a person's torso tends to be in proportion to the rest of their body, it's always a surprise when someone stands up and is taller than average. Especially if he then crosses his arms. This often happens in holding cells after trash-talking an inmate who's been crouching on the floor.

See: PRISON RAPE, HUMOROUS INTIMATIONS OF

# STOP

All good movies can be summarized as follows:

> We/I
> gotta
> STOP
> him/her/it/them.

The key is 'stop'. We want to see movies about people stopping shit. And then, after ninety minutes,[*] we want that shit to stop.

* Agreed. Nothing should last 157 minutes. That's longer than some labours – *Ayo*.

# STORY

What is a STORY? Why do we tell them to other people? How much time do they take? Would it be better to sit down just in case? Why are there other people?

Do all great stories overlap? Can a good story lap a bad story?

Are there certain patterns that underlie all narrative? Then why can't you knit them? Is it because you can only feel them? With what? Your heart? But what if your heart has stopped feeling? What if it's calcified, blackened, heavy with hate, gridlocking your throat, damming your saliva – what then? Who's going to help you? Your wife? Are you kidding? Don't you remember her running away with that waffle magnate?

These are all questions. Which makes us ask: what is a question?

For isn't a question a kind of story?

We are all One Story, revealing itself to itself, in an infinite river of consciousness.

But who owns the remake rights?

Probably Disney.*

But since we're here, and there's time left on the meter, let's

---

* But who owns Disney? Is it still that mouse? How is a mouse richer than me, a man? People used to say, 'What are you? A man or a mouse?' Who knew it would be better to be a mouse? – *Ayo.*

break story down to its rawest structural components. Let's take a tale that we all know and love. A superficially simple yarn that's stood the test of time:

The cat sat on the mat.

At first glance it seems to have everything: an interesting central character, a compellingly relatable central action sequence and a great location. But with a little grunt work we can make this story *even better.*

Let's *break it down* . . .

T
H
E

C
A
T

S
A
T

O
N

T
H
E

M
A
T

Woah there. That's too much. That's practically sub-atomic. Let's build it back up a touch:

THE CAT

SAT

ON THE MAT

Straight outta the gate we meet our HERO: a cat. Who is this cat? We don't know. What does (s)he want? A seat. (S)he so desperately wants to sit. What's the resolution? The cat achieves his/her goal with the help of a mat. The end.

There's no build-up, no context and no backstory! And when (s)he reaches his/her goal, we, as an audience, are denied the emotional catharsis we crave. We don't even know this cat's name!

Where are the stakes? Where is the drama? Why should we care? There are cats sat on mats up and down the country at any given moment – what makes this particular cat so special? What makes the story of *this cat* on *this mat* a story that we *need to tell*?

How could we improve this? We need to tackle the character of 'the cat'. Let's make the cat a male. Straight away I'm starting to relate. Let's call him Brad (Brad Pitt). What kind of cat is Brad? Maybe he's a cat from the wrong side of the tracks, a dreamer, but with street smarts – good-lookin' son of a bitch too. When he was a kitten his parents never believed he'd amount to anything. His talons only part retracted, he was slow to bury his feces and he hated string. 'You're gonna end up an alley cat like your uncle, Top,' they'd meow, as they nosed round one another's anal canals.

Then one day, while stripping flesh from a rodent, Brad looks up: it's the most beautiful thing he's ever seen. Rolled up, under the arm of a super-hot Cameron Diaz type, is a ruby-red mat.

He knows one thing for sure: he must sit on that mat.

So much for the set-up. Now for the complication.

The super-hot Cameron Diaz type lives uptown in a fancy town-house and only wears really tight clothing. She gets the doorman to set out the new mat. It looks beautiful. Brad's never seen a mat that even comes close. He struts up to it, tail a mile in the air. But right as he's about to park his ass for the afternoon, guess who sets up camp?

Camera tracks toward a tough-lookin' rough mutt called Rico. He's non-American, big scar down his face, one eye's kinda milky, barks with a thick accent. We immediately know this piece of shit's bad news, but for some reason the doorman loves him. Maybe they do coke together. We can sketch in the details later. Upshot? Ain't no way Brad's getting on that mat any time soon.

So Brad goes on a stake-out, trying to see if Rico operates any kind of mat schedule. He's joined by a wisecracking city fox, Franklin (Kevin Hart), who keeps undermining him: 'I'm tellin ya, man, that canine's a 24/7 deal. Wass tha' tatty-ass rug t'ya anyways? Yo' no-good broke ass too good for the flo'?'

The unlikely duo attempt to lure Rico off the mat using various methods (a sexy poodle, a juicy steak on a wire, etc.), but he ain't goin' no place no how. Somehow he always sees them coming. Cut to Cameron Diaz type in the shower. This has no real plot function, but why not shoot it just in case?

In despair, Brad the cat hits a local bar. Gets lit on milk punch. Wakes up in a dumpster. Staggers out, fur smeared with prawn tails. A group of mice beat him up for what he did to their uncle. He coughs up some cream. He's at ROCK BOTTOM. Even the moonlight hurts his eyes, so he picks some old shades out of the trash. He catches his reflection in a dirty puddle. What's different? That's it! Rico always saw him coming because cats' eyeballs have a special reflective layer called the *tapetum lucidum*! Of course!

He and Franklin both get sunglasses and decide to make their move. Only problem? Now they can't see where they're going. Cue a series of comic pratfalls that leads them straight to the city pound.

There they meet a wise old tortoise, Speedy McNulty (Morgan Freeman), who's serving time for tax evasion. With the help of a beautiful, feisty tabby cat, Miss Kitty (Jennifer Lawrence), the three of them break out, but McNulty loses his shell. There's a moving scene where McNulty explains that although – yes – he does look funny now, the shell formed part of his spine, so now he's going to die. 'Momma said I never had much backbone. I guess she was right.' Brad tells him that's bullshit, that McNulty has more backbone than anyone he's ever met. It just turns out that McNulty's backbone is detachable. But ain't no shame in that – that's just how Nature designed it. Just like she designed it so that dogs always win and cats always lose. McNulty tells Brad to never give up and, above all, be patient – he'll sit on that mat. He tells Franklin to go back to school – he has the makings of a fine lawyer. He tells Miss Kitty to stop her relentless killing spree – it's unfeminine.

Cut to the Cameron Diaz type back in the shower. You might need it in the edit.

Brad, Franklin and Miss Kitty try to crush McNulty's shell flat so that it'll fit in a shallow grave. But it won't break.

Which leads to our resolution.

The camera closes in on a tortoise shell scuttling fast.

We see Brad inside. I think we've got a pretty good idea where he's goin'.

As Brad finally sits on the mat, Rico wakes up from his snooze. What the hell is this shell doing on *his mat*?! Then Miss Kitty descends on Rico in a murderous flurry that finally sates her lifelong bloodlust. Miss Kitty is arrested. Franklin, with his new legal qualifications, wows the judge, who dismisses the charges against Miss Kitty and pins the killing on a transient Hispanic hamster.

Brad and Miss Kitty get married. Franklin's the best man. He buys them a brand-new red mat for their wedding present. Everyone applauds. Dissolve: the two of them with their wedding gift in front of their new townhouse. They stretch out on the mat together.

Tonight, they'll fuck on that mat.

Slam cut to credits.

See: AMERICA AS MAT; HERO, THE; ROCK BOTTOM

# SUSPENSE

Alfie Hitchcock.

Met the guy for a hot second. I was a struggling screenwriter; he was struggling to fit in his pants.* Yours truly had a story about some stiff correctly accused of something he didn't feel guilty about. I thought it could be a nice change of pace for Hitch; he could cast it with unknowns and shoot the fucker on the streets. It was pretty rough and in no way ready, but I managed to wangle a sit-down with the big guy for reasons that I'm not prepared to lay out in print.** So I washed up and cruised down to this high-class waffle joint, where I got primo service on account of the fact I had the waitress there on a maintenance fuck. She was actually a very special lady. I think her name had an 'L' in it. She definitely had gigantic tits. That I do remember.

Each time the door opened, my heart was in my mouth. Which, being filled with teeth, is no place for a heart. Unless you're a cannibal.*** But for personal reasons I was in one of my pescatarian phases**** and the only things I wanted in *my* mouth were

* *I'm* struggling to see the connection. I imagine a man as prepared as Hitchcock would've made sure he was stocked to the gills with jumbo pants – *Ayo*.

** One rumour I heard was that LaSure was able to do a very good Grace Kelly impression – *Ayo*.

*** I bet if you're a cannibal the heart is the best part, the thing you save for last – *Ayo*.

**** Whenever Gordy had blown all his dollar on rye, he would switch from meat tacos to fish tacos, figuring fish were free, whereas mince was for high rollers.

that waitress's gigantic tits.* Laverne? Maybe the waffles were making me think of tits. Or was I eating waffles because they reminded me of tits? You really can't beat tits or waffles. Why does life sometimes make us choose between them?

Kelsey? Ashlynn?

'Great,' I remember thinking, 'now I'm hard, and if I have to stand up to shake Hitch's hand, I'll probably flip the table with my massive whang.'

Laycee? Lola? Earlene?

And I thought about all the times when I'd been socially compromised by getting a giant boner, and wondered whether The Feminists ever took THAT into consideration when they were saying how tough life was for *them*. They ought to try living with sudden boners for thirty years!

Melody? Maybelle? Kayla? Lori?

So I ordered some rye to take the edge off, plus two rounds of corned-beef hash, which always seems to help me stop thinking too much about tits.

Crystal? Taylor? Darlene? Shelby? Something-Lynn?

And I was reminded of when Hitchcock famously said that if two people are talking in a restaurant and a bomb suddenly

---

He would go down to the LA aqueduct and steal the catches from local anglers, claiming to be a park ranger. The problem he faced was storage. As a lover of rye, ice could not be wasted, and he certainly couldn't afford to power a fridge – *Ayo*.
* I tried to suggest that the phrasing here has the disconcerting effect of making it sound like this waitress's breasts were 'fishy'. His voicemail response? 'Listen, fucker, there was nothing remotely fishy about those headrests! I trusted those things with my life!' – *Ayo*.

goes off, all you have are a few seconds of surprise, but if you see someone plant a bomb under the table and two people sit down at that table, you have SUSPENSE. So anyway, I thought it might be fun to rig up a fake bomb to put under the table. Luckily, I always keep a bunch of differently colored curly wires in my flak jacket, and I had a couple of dynamite sticks left over from summer. So I'm sitting there with my 'fake bomb', sweating off the rye and the beef and the waffles . . . but no Hitch!

Talk about suspense!

Finally, Hitch waltzes in, fifteen minutes late! He waddles over to me and says, 'Have you seen a blonde woman with a neat beehive?' So I say, 'Well, I guess this is one Hitch that *ain't* in time.'

I was of course referring to the hit proverb 'A Stich in Time Saves Nine', while also giving a tip of the hat to how much the word 'Hitch' sounds like 'stitch'. Fact was, Hitch was a very punctual man; indeed, he wasn't late at all. I had given him the WRONG time just so that I could make the pun! The poor sap didn't know where to look. He was going all red in the face (the exertion of walking up the stairs must've been catching up with him), and I had this eat-shit grin plastered on my kisser.

I decided to put him out of his misery and tell him that I wasn't Grace Kelly, and even if I were still willing to pretend to be, there was no way I could do the things I'd said I could on the phone. I expected him to double over with laughter, even though there was no way this guy could double over, he was that huge.

He spun round and left. Or maybe he left and then spun round. I was pretty soused, and I was so full up/horny I could barely focus. I could've been the one spinning round. Point is, he heaved his hefty heinie out of what must've been a specially widened door.

And if truth be doled, it was a mercy that he walked out then, because I wasn't really sure how to develop the pun into the 'saves nine'* part. Meaning if he'd got in my face and been all, 'How does my being slightly tardy – if indeed I am – relate to the idea of a timely action averting the unnecessary expenditure of energy in correcting an earlier error of omission?', I would've had to go, 'I gotta 'fess, Hitchie baby, I only had the first part of the wordplay sketched out, and any follow-up would have been something that happened in the moment depending on what you said.' So I started to wonder whether there was a more layered pun to be had – perhaps something centered around the word 'itch' – when someone shouted, 'Bomb! He's got a bomb!'

Next thing I know, there's a piece in my face and the cuffs go on.

Anyway, that was my time with Alfred Hitchcock!

That slob took my dreams.

But up until that moment, I'd felt more suspense than I'd felt watching any one of his peepy-pervy films.**

---

* Which, BTW, I've always found weird. How could they be so confident the ratio of 'saved' stitches to 'made' stitches would always be 1:9? I honestly think that ratio was only selected because it rhymes! And if we start living our lives simply on the basis of what rhymes, where will we draw the line(s)?(!) – *Ayo.*

** Whenever someone asks me which films are my 'guilty pleasure', I say, 'Hitchcock films' – cos that's exactly what they are – *Ayo.*

# SUSPENSION OF DISBELIEF

Every time you go into a movie theater you SUSPEND YOUR DISBELIEF.

How else would you get through it?

'Maybe this one will be good,' you think to yourself. 'I like that actor. He's sometimes okay. And that woman on the poster is attractive. I think she might even be of *above-average attractiveness*. She's looking at me in a very seductive way. If the circumstances were right, I think she could fall for me. Given time. And this whole franchise is getting richer and more complex with each new instalment. Didn't I read somewhere that superhero movies are the nineteenth-century novels of Our Time? I definitely read something that made a very compelling case for the value of superhero movies within The Culture. How they're mythic sagas, embodying storytelling that's been around since the dawn of narrative itself. That if Dickens were alive now, he'd be operating within the Marvel Universe.* And even though they *feel* like narcotizing pap designed to give the false illusion that life

---

* How can Marvel have its own universe? If the universe is All Time and Space and its Contents, wouldn't the Marvel Universe be contained within the universe in which I hitherto believed myself to exist? And wouldn't that make the Marvel Universe not a universe per se, but an aggressively policed set of intellectual property rights? And please don't start with the multiverse thing. It's bad enough that I was excluded from all the cool parties at school. Now you're telling me there are whole realities I can't access? – *Ayo.*

contains resolutions, they for some reason aren't.'*

Sure, baby. Whatever gets you through the next ninety.**

In most people's lives, the biggest suspension of disbelief comes right before you say, 'I do.'

But if you got real, what you'd really say is, 'I'd kind of like to, but I doubt I can.'

See: *MARVEL'S ORPHAN RISING: THE NEW ADVENTURES OF OLIVER TWIST*

---

* As opposed to relationships, which seem to operate under the laws of entropy: each time one breaks down, a little piece of you disappears – and no one can tell where that piece has gone – and that hole in your chest gets wider and wider until you wonder whether this is a cavity inside you or the infinite black of space! – *Ayo.*
** I wish. These days it takes films ninety minutes to warm up – *Ayo.*

# SUSPICIOUS NATIVE, THE

As the HERO pads toward him, fearless but respectful, we see revealed the SUSPICIOUS NATIVE, his face an onyx edifice, his moon-white eyes unable to comprehend.

In Joseph Zito's 1988 African-set counter-insurgency dramedy *Red Scorpion*, Nikolai Petrovitch Rachenko (Dolph Lundgren) is a Soviet agent who loses faith in commie high command. He flees to the desert and, dehydrated, passes out. Native bushmen find his body and take him to their village, but before long they're laughing at him for being unable to spear a warthog! But why should Rachenko be able to spear a warthog? He's white! He buys his food in shops like a normal person! He could buy a billion warthogs in Whole Foods!

But Rachenko doesn't respond to their mockery. He doesn't try and undermine them. He could easily say, 'Maybe if you people had industrialized, we'd be bolt-gunning warthogs in a slaughterhouse like civilized people.' Instead, he calmly sets about proving Nietzsche right. Not only does he *easily* spear a warthog after a matter of *days*, but he also learns how to say the words 'thank' and 'you' in their native tongue. This is a Renaissance Man. Which they'd know if they'd even *had a* Renaissance! They couldn't tell a Renaissance Man if, to the accompaniment of crumhorn and lute, he challenged them to a joust in a palazzo while a Flemish portraitist captured the scene in realistic linear perspective!

'You've earned the mark of the hunter,' the Village Elder says in his barely comprehensible dialect. He gives Rachenko a long spear, immunity to scorpions and a tattoo on his left tit.

'I've come a long way,' Rachenko replies with contrasting humility.

Too fuckin' right! I'd love to see the Village Elder attain Rachenko's level of expertise in a similarly short montage!

But sometimes a suspicious native will mutter an aphorism in the middle of Act II that will resonate later in Act III, allowing the hero to display HIS INHERENT MORAL SUPERIORITY. In Alejandro G. Iñárritu's 2015 man vs bear grudge match *The Revenant*,* Pawnee refugee Hikuc (Arthur RedCloud) tells maul victim Hugh Glass** (Leonardo DiCaprio) that 'Revenge is in the Creator's hands.' Later, having pummeled near-incomprehensible trapper John Fitzgerald (Tom Hardy) by a riverbank, Glass remembers Hikuc's words and withholds a final death blow, instead pushing Fitzgerald across the water toward a patrol of suspicious natives, who, true to form, scalp the fucker.

See: HERO, THE; INHERENT MORAL SUPERIORITY OF THE HERO, THE; SCALPING DOS AND DON'TS

---

* AKA the most expensive Bear Grylls episode ever made – *Ayo*.
** I'm ashamed to admit that had he been to my school, he may have been teased for that name – *Ayo*.

T

*'And this is the clincher . . .'*

# TAGLINES

A TAGLINE is a short piece of text, often displayed on a movie poster, hinting at the key themes/aspects of the story. But it's amazing how often these marketing goons get it wrong.

Take Ingmar Bergman's 1968 sedative *Hour of the Wolf*:

> *The Hour of the Wolf is the hour between night and dawn. It is the hour when most people die, when sleep is deepest, when nightmares are most real. It is the hour when the sleepless are haunted by their deepest fear, when ghosts and demons are most powerful. The Hour of the Wolf is also the hour when most children are born.*

That ain't a *tagline*, it's a Wikipedia entry. It reminds me of when my last wife started talking. Terror would rise up in my throat. I knew I was meant to 'remain present', but how can you be 'present' if you don't know where the fuck you are? Where are the handles on this thing? At least give a sense of how long this is gonna take. It's just one thing after another. State your thesis, then support it: that's a conversation. I started trying to alternate my gaze between her eyes and her mouth and saying 'uh huh' every five seconds, but I'd feel my head get heavy, and before I could say 'shit' I'd be asleep at the wheel.

Bergman's previous catastrophe, *Persona*, ain't much better. Here's the tag:

*The new film by Ingmar Bergman.*

That's the best thing they could find to say about it. That it wasn't the last one. Maybe you know the plot? Two dames stuck on an island, but only one of them talks. Please. I like sci-fi, but give me something halfway credible.

In John Irvin's 1986 Mafia dramedy *Raw Deal*, Mark Kaminsky (Arnold Schwarzenegger) is a wrongly dismissed FBI agent who infiltrates the Mob to tear them a new one from right under their feet. Tagline?

*The system gave him a raw deal. Nobody gives him a raw deal.*

But the system literally just GAVE him a raw deal. Why should I see your movie if you're lying to me already?

In Joseph Zito's 1988 counter-insurgency saga *Red Scorpion*, Nikolai Petrovitch Rachenko (Dolph Lundgren) is an elite Soviet soldier who infiltrates the commies in Africa to tear them a new one from the inside out. Tagline?

*He's a human killing machine. Taught to stalk. Trained to kill. Programmed to destroy. He's played by their rules . . . Until now.*

Get out your little red pen, boy. Isn't it obvious that a human killing machine will have been 'trained to kill'? Even Stallone didn't come out of the womb busting heads. And 'programmed to destroy' is the same as 'trained to kill'! I want to kill whoever wrote this! Unless they also wrote 'Taught to stalk', which is pretty much the best ordering of any three words ever, except for 'You're all clear'.

In David Cronenberg's overhyped 1986 insect dramedy *The Fly*, scientist Seth Brundle (Jeff Goldblum) inadvertently fuses himself with the titular in a teleporter. Hilarity ensues. Yet the tagline is:

*Be afraid. Be very afraid.*

Of what? Bug spray? And by the way, you don't need the first statement. 'Afraid' is a subset of 'very afraid': you can't be 'very afraid' without being 'afraid'. And you've used the word 'be' twice. If this tag's anything to go by, you could lose 40 per cent of the movie without even noticing.

Harley Cokeliss's 1987 Burt Reynolds-starring procedural *Malone* has this appeal for your custom:

*Ex-cop. Ex-CIA. Ex-plosive.*

So this former law-enforcement officer also used to be a 'plosive'? What was he? The letter 'b'? Had a little alphabetical reassignment and now he's pursuing a new life as a sibilant? Cos I'm not sure I'm ready for *Sesame Street Undercover* . . .

In Michael Miller's 1982 kung fu sci-fi[*] drama *Silent Rage*, a small-town sheriff must destroy a mentally ill man granted near indestructibility by a botched experiment. Here's the tag:

*Science created him. Now Chuck Norris must destroy him.*

What was the experiment in? Meta-textuality? Chuck Norris is the talented actor *playing* Sheriff Dan Stevens. Why would you confuse them?

The copy for Roger Donaldson's 1988 bartender dramedy *Cocktail* is:

[*] Sci-fu? – *Ayo.*

*When he pours, he reigns.*

But since when does being a bartender confer sovereignty? The idea that working in the catering industry might lead to some kind of monarchical power is completely misleading and lost me the best part of a summer. My suggestion:

DO *mix your drinks.*

*Jaws: The Revenge* goes with:

*This time it's personal.*

I can be touchy, but of all the things to take personally, a shark attack isn't one of them. Speaking from experience, you've got no one to blame but yourself.

Orson Welles's 1941 ass-backward jumble *Citizen Kane* has a tag that's even more misguided than the movie:

*It's terrific!*

That's what you say if someone gives you a jumper you hate. Here's how to do it right:

*Welles, Welles, Welles.*

Let's close with a coupla stone-face killers.

In Bruno Barreto's 2003 cabin-crew drama *View from the Top,*[*] Donna Jensen (Gwyneth Paltrow) plays a small-town girl striving to become a first-class international flight attendant. The tagline?

---

[*] At the risk of committing a meta-textual breach of my own, I re-refer interested readers to my own treatise on this masterful movie, 'Ayoade on *View from the Top*: A Modern Masterpiece' – *Ayo.*

*Don't stop till you reach the top.*

Grade A+. This is going to be an exhilarating tale of raw, Darwinian ambition. Relentless and thrillingly linear.

And this is the clincher. Mike Nichols's 1973 aqua-com *The Day of the Dolphin* dropped this dangler:

> *Unwittingly, he trained a dolphin to kill the President of the United States.*

This tagline was so fully satisfying as a piece of work in its own right that no one felt the need to see the movie.

See: IMPOSSIBILITY OF REMAINING PRESENT, THE

# TAKING PUNCHES FROM
# HYSTERICAL WOMEN

In most cases the HERO should just stand there and take them. The woman's clearly upset and not in her right mind. She might be bereaved or think that something's the hero's fault. She just needs time. Very often they're barely punches at all, more like half-slaps/pushes, and she instinctively knows not to touch his hair.

In most instances someone with a bit of sense will drag her off, whereupon she's reduced to mere verbal insults or a Spit From Distance.

Heroes are used to being spat on. Comes with the territory. You and I might go, 'Ew!!! That was totally gross and really un-hygienic actually.' But the hero will simply remove the spittle with nothing more than the back of his hand and a rueful smile.

However, there are times when he is justified in slapping a HYSTERICAL WOMAN back:

1. She's getting even more hysterical.
2. They could be overheard by enemy snipers.
3. She needs to shape up before the building explodes.

See: HERO, THE; SLAPPING DOS AND DON'TS

# THANKS

The HERO wants very little. A simple word of thanks, not that he'll ask for it, is his only recompense for saving Humanity. It's Mankind's inability to appreciate the hero that keeps him in exile, alone and often divorced.

In Joseph Zito's 1988 counter-insurgency drama *Red Scorpion*, Nikolai Petrovitch Rachenko (Dolph Lundgren) is an elite Soviet soldier who selflessly helps a rebel group overturn a corrupt commie regime in the Dark Continent. Not only do people fail to thank him for his efforts for much of the film but, understandably, they don't trust him because he's Russian, which in movie terms makes him a Foreign National.

But through his unique talent for destroying life he comes to win the respect and, ultimately, thanks of his peers. Looking like he's been formed in a particle collider containing the original line-up of Bros and two miles of tendon, Lundgren's character surveys the scorched scene of his PROLONGED ACT III ASS-KICK, when Kallunda Kintash (Al White), an African (representing savages everywhere), and Dewey Ferguson (M. Emmet Walsh), an American (representing the pinnacle of the civilized free world), take a moment to offer their approbation:

```
    KALLUNDA KINTASH (THE AFRICAN)
We made it, my friend.
```

                DEWEY FERGUSON (THE AMERICAN)
You did it, man.


                NIKOLAI PETROVITCH RACHENKO
                        (THE RUSSIAN)
Fuckin' A.


This simple, moving exchange shows how far each has come on
their unique journeys. But note that only the American has the
graciousness – a noted characteristic of his people – to single out
someone else's achievement. In *Red Scorpion*, as in all good movies, the true victory is for the INHERENT SUPERIORITY
OF THE AMERICAN WAY.

See: ASS-KICK, PROLONGED ACT III; THE AMERICAN WAY,
INHERENT SUPERIORITY OF; THE DARK CONTINENT,
IMPORTANCE OF KEEPING A FIRM HAND ON THE TILLER
W/R/T; GRACIOUSNESS, UNIQUELY AMERICAN MODES OF;
HERO, THE

# THOUGHT

The only method of conveying THOUGHT in cinema is to bookend a series of fragmented, desaturated flashback images with a close-up shot of someone's strained-looking face.

And that ain't gonna change any time soon. Unless . . .

    *Camera tracks into my face. Dissolve*
    *to . . .*

# TIMING

In movies, TIMING is the key to everything.

Except for locks.

For locks you need a key.

# TITLES

The TITLE of your picture should be intriguing and exciting, but it should let the audience know *exactly* what to expect. As such, *Beverly Hills Cop* may be the best movie title of all time. But it's a question of nuance. As tempting as it feels, you can't just put 'Cop' after another noun and expect a flick to be a hit . . .

*Kindergarten Cop*
How dangerous is day care? Why does it need policing? Are these babies carrying handguns? Too many questions.

*Mall Cop*
If you say it out loud, it sounds like someone telling a dog to disembowel a detective.

*Cop Out*
So he's gay. Why do I care?

*Cop and a Half*
Of soy? What is this, a movie or a recipe?

But if you come up with a kick-butt title like *RoboCop*, your work is pretty much done. All you gotta do next is think of a story to back it up. And remember: no cinema offers refunds based on quality; you just need to get 'em through the door.

# TITS

. . . are a mixed blessing.

In Tobe Hooper's 1985 space-vampire dramedy *Lifeforce*, an astronaut considers removing the modesty sheet from a beautiful dead humanoid in order to take a respectful look at her jugs. But before he can get a proper eyeful, she sits up and sucks all the life out of him.[*]

Here we see a microcosm of the sexual act: anticipation, consummation, fatal depletion.

Hooper's brilliantly prescient film is a timely warning about the transfixing power of wallopers.

See: TOWEL RACKS

---

[*] One of those undead, intergalactic honeytraps – *Ayo*.

# TOPLESSNESS

Actresses often complain that certain producers pressure them to 'appear topless' in certain films, when in fact they are merely being asked to expose their breasts.

Film is a visual medium. If an actress 'appeared topless', what would we look at? Some disembodied legs?

In the entire history of motion pictures, a pair of disembodied legs has rarely managed to achieve movie-star status, whereas women wise enough to expose their breasts often become major stars.

So it's really a choice between bisecting yourself horizontally or getting work.

See: FEMINISM

# TRUST

'Trust me' is another way of saying, '*You* don't know what the hell you're doing, but *I* sure as shit do.'

HEROES don't got time for 'due process'. Things are getting too ugly, too fast for them to weigh up the moral complexities of torture. Their guts are calibrated to invariably make the right decision, even if it might seem to the untrained eye that a lot of people have started to lose their lives as a result of this revenge mission.

In Antoine Fuqua's 2014 home-depot dramedy *The Equalizer*, ex-CIA operative Robert 'Bob' McCall (Denzel Washington) decides to avenge a brutal assault on a prostitute he innocently befriended at a diner. With each particular kill he has to use his own judgment as to the level of force required, whether it's exploding a series of trucks, electrocution, strangulation, stabbing, shooting, or forcing a shot glass into someone's brain. It's a matter of discretion, but the level of force required often seems to be: A LOT.

Note: in the course of a revenge mission, it's permissible to take ANYTHING from ANYONE and DESTROY ANY and ALL THINGS.

See: CONFISCATION, HERO'S IMPLICITLY WIDE-RANGING POWERS OF; HERO, THE

# TWO-STAGE BAR BRIBES

TWO-STAGE BAR BRIBES (incl. shoe-shine/street-corner bribes) come in three stages:

Stage 1. HERO asks for info; snitch says, 'Who wants to know?'; hero offers 'x' dollar(s); brief comic business w/r/t value of 'x'; handover of 'x' dollar(s) (often folded); informant gives indication that he may know something but will prob need more dollar(s) to be sure.

Stage 2. Transfer of supplementary dollar(s) – 'y'; some (minor) info revealed; informant asks for yet more dollar(s) – 'z'.

Stage 3. Enraged/saddened by request for 'z' dollar(s), as a breach of an implied two-stage bar-bribe contract, hero commences COLLAR GRAB, accompanied w/ coarse threats (e.g. 'Listen, you fuck knuckle/Don't fuck with me, Chico,' etc.), to extract further intel; further intel is duly spilt; hero strongly requests additional intel spill; snitch says words to effect of 'That's all I know, man, I swear'; hero unhands scum-bucket; scum-bucket remonstrates w/r/t severity of collar grab; hero follows up lead in next scene.

More recently, the Two-Stage Bar Bribe scene has been replaced by the torture scene, in which the hero may extract intel by methods incl. (but not limited to) Single Gunshot to a Non-Fatal Body Area; Knife Twist; Digit Snap; Chinese Burn (Severe);

Window Dangle; Pushing Informant's Head Toward Something That Would Fatally Damage Informant's Head, i.e. drill, band saw, electric whisk, etc.

I welcome this shift, as I was always uncomfortable with lowlife scum getting dollar for intel that could be just as easily extracted by moving straight to Stage 3.

See: HERO, THE; PAY, WHY

# U

*'We must deceive ourselves
in order to go on . . .'*

# UK FILM

'It's been an outstanding year in UK film . . .' is the claim the UK film 'industry' continues to make to itself on an annual basis, fundamentally perverting the definition of the word 'outstanding', bankrupting language itself and destroying trust in that most sacred of spheres: PR. Far better to say, 'It's been a year,' and leave it at that. For the UK FILM industry is, like the unicorn, a myth: something that is fun to imagine, but impossible to believe in.

Yet, in show business, we must deceive ourselves in order to go on. To us, lying to ourselves is as natural as (briefly) marrying people half our age.

Case in point: that last sentence contained a deception. I used the term 'show business', two words which don't apply to UK film. Because for something to be a 'show', people have to watch it. And for something to be a business . . . well, I guess the end of that sentence writes itself.

Not that I'm bitter – I live abroad now.

On a side note, it's important never to applaud people 'working' in UK film, as it may startle them. They are unused to applause, coming as it does from audiences. People 'working' in UK film have rarely heard any sounds from an audience other than dry coughs.*

* Or a murmured suggestion to leave, followed by the awkward 'thuk' of a cinema seat flipping back up – *Ayo*.

At UK film 'events', they often have an award for the Best International Film. This film, by its very definition, is always better than the 'Best' UK film because the Best International Film will be American. In fact, the Best International Film won't be a film at all: it'll be a movie.

A movie is a film people want to watch.

Having a category for Best International Film is like having a special category for Best Tall Basketball Player of the Year. Conversely, you would never have an award for Whitest Athlete. That award is for tennis.

See: BRITISH FILM

# V

*'If we could take these lessons
into the school system . . .'*

# VILLAINS

VILLAINS rarely have top lips.

Villains like fruit-based cocktails.

Villains like fussy food.

Villains struggle to maintain team spirit.

Villains struggle with stress management, and tend to unload onto subordinates.

Villains set themselves unrealistic goals.

Villains, by their nature, tend not to be American.

Villains are obsessed with failure, yet they never succeed.

HEROES don't worry about failure, yet they always succeed.

Perhaps if these lessons could have been taken into the school system, I wouldn't have left without qualifications.

See: HERO, THE

*'The answer's simple . . .'*

# WHEN VS WHETHER

When we're watching a good movie, we know what's gonna happen. That's why they're comforting. If you'd told me thirty years ago that I'd be single and living most of my life in a jeep, I wouldn't have paid the price of admission.

So with the flicks that matter it ain't a question of WHETHER, it's a question of WHEN ...

WHEN will Steven Seagal break someone's arm by bending it the wrong way at the elbow?

WHEN will Nicolas Cage start screaming?

WHEN will Robert De Niro do that thing with his mouth?*

There are too many surprises in life; we don't need 'em in drama.

---

* I have my own set of WHENs:
  WHEN will Liam Neeson's daughter in *Taken* realise how dangerous gap years are?
  WHEN will the Albanian Mafia realise that Liam Neeson is more powerful than all of them put together?
  WHEN will Sean Penn realise that everyone gets cut out of Terrence Malick films in favour of those prepared to skip through meadows?
  WHEN will Nic Cage realise that it's possible for a character to get *moderately* annoyed? – *Ayo.*

# WISECRACKS

All humor comes out of a fear of mortality, which is why the death of an enemy is an excellent time to test out new material and lighten the mood before the next kill.

See: KILLING SPREE, SETTING THE RIGHT ATMOSPHERE ON A

# WOMEN

I think men and WOMEN are different. My female students work *better* if I flatter them and give them mix tapes and praise their poetry. (The pretty ones, at least. There's always a couple of tanks who try to stir shit up cos they don't got a date to the prom.) Whereas the more I belittle the men (boys, really) and say that I *would* let them ride in my car if it wasn't so full of high-class ass, the better *they* seem to do. It's just an evolutionary fact. If you wanna get mad, get mad at Chuck Darwin.*

But the bottom line is that without women, there would be no movies. Who else would we mentally undress? Who else would we rescue? Who else would we lovingly but firmly tell to stay put while we get on with the DANGEROUS ASS-KICKING BUSINESS OF ACT III?

But that's not to say women are just passengers. Sometimes dames can help – e.g. by smashing something light/breakable over someone's head, thus giving the leading man a little extra time to deal with the other assailants.

See: ACT III, THE DANGEROUS ASS-KICKING BUSINESS OF

---

* I've always wondered whether Chuck D's name was a reference to Darwin – *Ayo*.

# WORD, GIVING IT

When the HERO GIVES his WORD, it ain't like a groom saying, 'I do.' This gift ain't just for Christmas, it's till the final credits roll. And just like your momma's hymen, you should think twice before breaking it.

Perhaps that's why so many heroes choose to speak in grunts.

Grunts don't break.

See: HERO, THE; INHERENT UNBREAKABILITY OF
GRUNTS, THE; YOUR MOMMA'S HYMEN, IMPORTANCE OF
RESPECT VIS-À-VIS

# WORDPLAY

Félix Enríquez Alcalá's 1997 eco-thriller *Fire Down Below* is rightly renowned as a WORDPLAY masterclass. Let's break down two key exchanges.

In the first, undercover CIA operative Jack Taggart (Steven Seagal) comes face to face with the villainous Hanner Sr (Kris Kristofferson):

```
          HANNER SR
  You're violating my constitutional rights.


          JACK TAGGART
  I will show you a new meaning to the word
  'violation'.
```

Apart from the filmmakers' evident joy at the possibilities of language, what's truly interesting is that Taggart *isn't* going to show Hanner Sr a new meaning to the word 'violation'. Seagal's signature smirk tells us that the activity he's implying would still fall under the umbrella term 'violation'. Indeed, for the threat to work, Hanner Sr is required to *imagine* the kind of violation that Taggart is suggesting. And if we assume that the violation would be non-consensual – and I think it's safe to assume that it *would* be non-consensual – what we're talking about here is quite clear.

This is a rape threat.

And 'rape' is one of the possible definitions of 'violation'. So what Taggart's going to show Hanner Sr is an *existing* meaning of the word 'violation'. And while it may be hard to say for sure whether he's *personally* threatening to rape Hanner Sr, Taggart does seem to be leaving that possibility open.

Here's another way that the scene *could* have been written, if screenwriters Jeb Stuart and Philip Morton had a less sure hand with subtext:

HANNER SR
You're violating my constitutional rights.

JACK TAGGART
I'm going to rape you.

Not quite as witty, is it? It lacks *wordplay*. Action films of the late eighties and early nineties seem to be the only forum left in which a Man's Man like Seagal could, inspired by a sheer love of language, threaten to rape another man. Then the PC brigade rode in on their holier-hobby-horses-than-thou, leaving the battlefield strewn with harmless banter, making the movies a much poorer place as a result. They're certainly a whole heap less fun, and I think repressing people's freedom to threaten male rape as a punishment may be turning everyone gay. I don't know. You can't say anything now without people twisting your words. People will probably start calling me a homophobe just because I happen to find gayness terrifying.

In our next featured scene Taggart is undertaking some routine reconnaissance when he's intercepted by villainous flunky Hatch (Mark Collie):

                    HATCH
What the hell are you doing here?


                 JACK TAGGART
Well, I was just out taking a Sunday
stroll . . . but I guess maybe it's not
Sunday.


This guy's too much! Hatch was probably thinking, 'That's weird – it's not Sunday. This guy is out of his idiomatic depth,' when – BOOM! – Taggart calls him on it. 'But I guess maybe it's not Sunday,' he says, casual as shit. What do you think of that rejoinder, you low-level flunky fuck? This ain't some meathead you're dealing with. You're face to face with a master of repartee!

And the linguistic light show ain't about to dim. See how Taggart subtly *qualifies* the qualifier: 'But I *guess maybe* it's not Sunday.'

So maybe it *is* Sunday!

Who knows? You think this killing machine checks his iCal alerts? He's too busy snatching guns out of drug dealers' outstretched hands. You think Taggart has a Stroll Schedule? Taggart strolls to his own completely unpredictable and heavily syncopated rhythm. He'll take a Tuesday Stroll on a weekend. He'll take a mid-morning nap in the dead of night. His breathing pattern is so unusual it's hard to know how far through a sentence he is.

Upshot? Hatch can no longer tell one day from another! And Taggart hasn't even started physically assaulting him!

This is wordplay *in action*.

See: iCAL ALERTS, KILLING MACHINES' INSOUCIANCE W/R/T

# WORK

How do we know if a film works?

When I was a wee laddie, mid-mooch along the Celtic cobbles of East Kilbride, dreaming of new foodstuffs to submerge in hot oil, I thought WORK was something you tried to avoid. 'I dinnae wanna werk!' I'd oft exclaim to my young Scotch friends, many of them already parents, faces shrunken, smocks smeared with dirt, darting black eyes searching for escape. Aye, work was for 'gingin' fannybawbags'. Strictly for the spondoolies. But what that little braveheart couldnae have predicted was that one day he would *live* for work. And what's more, a whole Town would be gobbling up his pamphlets like bone-in picnic ham.

But this is noun talk. We need to get verb-al.

As in . . .

### WORK, v.

So you could say that the opening paragraph to this chapter was completely unnecessary, and you'd be right – it was an irrelevance. Worse, it was a prologue.

With prose you can scribble any old 'gash' and it's 'nae bother' . . .

But movies are an *art*. They don't sell them at *airports*. They have to be slicker than an unregulated-factory shoreline.

Remember the start to *2001: A Space Odyssey*? Bunch of monkeys collecting bones. What's that got to do with space? They don't even have lasers!

Cut that shit.

And what about *Citizen Kane*? A guy so drunk he can't hold onto a snow globe mutters something about the clitoris and then dies for no reason. Suddenly, we're into a ten-minute news bulletin that schleps through his entire life story, then we're back in the future with a bunch of silhouettes arguing about what he said when he died, even though no one could have heard it, plus who gives a shit, and then we have to go through the whole thing again starting from his childhood! No wonder they couldn't get distribution. If they'd wanted to gross some dollar, they should've called it *Dude, Where's My Sled*?

So how do we know if a film works?

The answer's simple. One word.

The audience.

The audience tell you. They'll whisper it in your ears as you try to get to sleep. ('Hey, Orson! I want my spondoolies back! The sled was in storage the whole time!')

Never disrespect your audience. They barely have any self-respect to start with. If they did, they'd be reading a book.

Just like you've been . . .

# FADE
# OUT

*'You know there's a special name
for that kind of "grip" . . .'*

The clouds fill, the rains fall, but the sea remains, as does some land.

A cycle without end or beginning. Which makes scheduling tough.

So, too, the movies.

They go on.

Sweet mercy, they go on. Do they think we have all day?

But what of those regions of cinema that have been hosed down the delta of 'progress'?

What of the heterosexual buddy film, kung fu films starring white people, and sincere slasher films?

Perhaps their day has sailed.

Well, not in my backyard.

This landlubber is itching to pilot them back to his private dock.

So, what of the future? Will the waves be calm? Or choppy as shit? Will this book help us stay on course? Why would you even say that? Don't put your negativity on me – I didn't promise anything sober.

All *I've* done is tell you exactly how every movie that has ever been good *works*. All *you* have to do is copy the formula.

The only thing stopping you is dumb pride.

You see it different? Great, have a margarita. *You* chart the course, I'll grab a dinghy. I'd rather paddle ashore with my rancid tongue.

Because come the apocalypse, the first thing us survivors will do, right after we thrash out a barter system for guzzolene, is tell one another *what happened* . . .

In other words, we'll start to tell *a story* . . .

Maybe get a couple of good-lookin' people to act it out . . .

Next thing you know, some guy in a checked shirt and baseball cap wants to make a *record* of that story . . .

Perhaps a *visual* record (heck, why not throw in some sound while we're at it) . . .

Then he can *show it to others* for a fee in selected theaters, and after a rapidly diminishing hold-back period, on home-entertainment platforms . . .

And if he wants people to keep watching and not start posting negative feedback on social media, that visual record had better hold them in its *grip* . . .

You know there's a special name for that kind of 'grip', right . . .?

I kinda coined it.

You just read it.

It's called . . .

# THE
# GRIP
# OF
# FILM

# INDEX*

* **BOLD CAPS** indicate a chapter heading. NON-BOLD CAPS indicate a deleted chapter heading – *Ayo*.

# OTHER PUBLICATIONS BY GORDY LaSURE

*Getting Creative with Gordy LaSure*

What is creativity? What does it mean to be creative? Aren't these two sentences essentially asking the same question? How can we translate creativity into something less useless, like money?

Gordy LaSure traces the history of creativity, from the Incas to Enrique Iglesias.

*So You Think You Can Think?*

What does it mean to have a thought?

How can you tell you're having a financially valuable one?

At what stage should you share this 'thought' with others? When a lawyer is present? Who's to say you can trust this 'lawyer'? Can you really trust a lawyer who advertises on the side of his truck? And how come your lawyer is moonlighting as a pest-control technician?

Gordy LaSure thumbs Thought's Crack wide open in this mind-defying pamphlet.

## Thinking First, Question Last

What does it mean to have a notion? Can you have half a notion? Can you copyright an inkling? What is the smallest but still fiscally significant percentile of an inkling?

In this breakthrough audio file, Gordy LaSure thrillingly trains you to commodify a thought before you even knew you had one.


## Channeling Your Inner Wind

We all know we can't build a kingdom from sub-particles of inklings, but how can we construct a character that gives the illusion of partial humanity? By using the Wind inside us, the painful, deeply private Wind we've had since childhood, and turning that trapped Wind into a calming, healing breeze.

In this challenging new PDF, Gordy LaSure will help fashion you a new kind of rope, enabling you to lasso your own unique gusts.

# CREDITS

*Quotations appear in the text from the screenplays of the following films:*

*Raw Deal* (1986), story by Luciano Vincenzoni and Sergio Donati; screenplay by Gary DeVore and Norman Wexler.

*Fire Down Below* (1997), story by Jeb Stuart; screenplay by Jeb Stuart and Philip Morton.

*Lawrence of Arabia* (1962), screenplay by Robert Bolt and Michael Wilson, based on *Seven Pillars of Wisdom* by T. E. Lawrence.

*Road House* (1989), story by R. Lance Hill (as David Lee Henry); screenplay by R. Lance Hill (as David Lee Henry) and Hilary Henkin.

*3 Days to Kill* (2014), story by Luc Besson; screenplay by Adi Hasak and Luc Besson.

*Timecop* (1994), story by Mark Verheiden; screenplay by Mark Verheiden and Mike Richardson, based on *Timecop* by Mike Richardson and Mark Verheiden.

*The Avengers* (2012), story by Zak Penn and Joss Whedon; screenplay by Joss Whedon, based on *The Avengers* by Stan Lee and Jack Kirby. (In the passage titled 'ACTORS, AMATEUR', the line 'Loki, turn off the Tesseract or I'll destroy it' is also from *The Avengers*.)

*The Revenant* (2015), screenplay by Mark L. Smith and Alejandro G. Iñárritu, based on *The Revenant* by Michael Punke.